RIGHT ON THE MONEY

Messages for Spiritual Growth Through Giving

Brian K. Bauknight

DISCIPLESHIP RESOURCES

MATERIALS FOR GROWTH IN CHRISTIAN FAITH & LIFE

— Nashville, Tennessee —

❖ TO PLACE AN ORDER OR TO INQUIRE ABOUT RESOURCES AND CUSTOMER ACCOUNTS, CONTACT:

DISCIPLESHIP RESOURCES DISTRIBUTION CENTER
P.O. BOX 6996
ALPHARETTA, GEORGIA 30239-6996

TEL: (800) 685-4370

FAX: (404) 442-5114

❖ FOR EDITORIAL INQUIRIES AND RIGHTS AND PERMISSIONS REQUESTS, CONTACT:

DISCIPLESHIP RESOURCES EDITORIAL OFFICES
P.O. BOX 840
NASHVILLE, TENNESSEE 37202-0840

TEL: (615) 340-7068

Cover concept and photo by John S. Cummings.

Library of Congress Catalog Card No. 93-70967

ISBN 0-88177-122-8

Unless otherwise indicated, all scripture quotations are taken from the New Revised Standard Version of the Holy Bible, © 1989 by the Division of Christian Education of the National Council of Churches of Christ in the USA and used by permission.

DR122

Contents

Preface v

Introduction vii

Part I: BASIC CHRISTIAN FORMATION 1

    1. Right on the Money! 3
    2. First Things First 9
    3. Knowing When to Tear Up Your Pledge Card 16
    4. Bounty Hunt 23
    5. The Sounds of Substance 29
    6. Good Growth Giving 36

Part II: TOWARD TITHING 43

    7. Fit to Be Tithed 45
    8. Blest Be the Tithe That Binds 50
    9. Tithes and Offerings 55
   10. Sermon on the Amount 62

Part III: CAPITAL CAMPAIGNS 69

   11. Worthy Visions 71
   12. A Farsighted People 76

Part IV: WORDS OF ENCOURAGEMENT 81

   13. Talent Search 82
   14. Always Abounding 88
   15. Energized Eagerness 93
   16. Possibilities in the Midst of Leanness 97

Endnotes 102

For Elaine,
who has taught me so much about the joy
of a spontaneous, giving spirit

Preface

This is a book about learning, living, and preaching stewardship. It is a tool for Christian formation in a very important discipline. As such, it is an offering to the church.

Many persons have been mentors to me over at least two decades in a formative theology of Christian giving. Most of those mentors are not even aware of the impact they have had. I am grateful to Lyle Schaller, Herb Miller, Ashley Hale, and Hilbert Berger in particular. Their books, articles, papers, and personal counsel have been invaluable.

Beyond these four, I am also enormously grateful to some marvelous laypersons who have taught me much about giving habits, about giving encouragement, and about personal contact for the express purpose of raising the sights of growing Christian disciples. These lay people have taught me to be direct, to ask for what is needed, to always present good information, and to challenge some of them to the distinct "gift of giving" as their particular response to God's call. To these persons, then, I have a special debt of gratitude. May their number increase, and may they help others as they have helped me.

I eagerly dedicate this book to my wife, Elaine. In more ways than I can possibly count, she has lifted me toward spontaneous giving and, as a result, the practice of living out some fresh dimension of discipleship. I have always known the "duty" of giving as a Christian and lover of the church. My wife has been a friend and an encourager on the broader journey of joyful giving.

This book, however, is mostly about financial giving through the church as an active act of faithfulness to our call. I continue to grow, to know a boldness in the gospel, and to be convinced that money is not some dreaded topic for the church, but rather integral to a holistic exercise of a vibrant faith.

Brian Kelley Bauknight
Pittsburgh, Pennsylvania
Lent 1993

Introduction

The most important challenge confronting the church of Jesus Christ is the formation of Christian disciples in the face of the steady encroachment of the secular. The gradual secularization of life is not necessarily evil in and of itself, but it clutters our vision and clouds the important disciplines that are necessary for a growing and relevant faith. In this book, I offer messages which focus upon a single imperative for vital discipleship: the need for eager, cheerful, financial contributors to the work of the kingdom of God.

Churches seem to regularly dread the issue of financial stewardship campaigns, or even the mention of money. The dread comes from both pulpit and pew. Pastors become awkward in the face of the annual ordeal of telling the faithful they need to give more. And the people resist the seeming intrusion into their private lives. Frequently, the matter of money is only endured. Seldom is it deemed an opportunity for refreshment and renewal.

In too many situations, the matter is simply never addressed in any significant way at all. Perhaps the reasons lie in the fear of rejection on the part of the pastor or leader. Perhaps there is concern for the loss of members over "too much talk about money." The matter of solid financial undergirding for the ministry of the church is reserved only for agonizing monthly agendas of finance committees, trustees, or a small advisory body hastily called to meet in the pastor's study. As a result, spiritual lives stagnate at a very critical point of Christian formation.

This book is one attempt to reverse (or, at least, to make a course correction) in that scenario. Contained in these pages are messages on the topic of money developed over more than a decade of ministry. They reflect texts and titles which seek to lift the subject of money to a new level, and which have the primary goal of Christian formation in both preacher and laity.

Some themes in the messages deserve brief introductory remarks. I have included those at the beginning of certain message groupings. However, at least four broad principles have guided the development of these messages over the years.

First, messages about money should be presented without apology. Too often, clergy begin speaking about money by defending themselves and the necessary burden of the subject. A few preachers openly admit that they hate to speak on the subject and do not look forward to the annual drive to raise the financial undergirding for the year. Some clergy insist that they simply cannot participate in a "program" to raise their own salaries every year. This book is based on the unalterable conviction that finances and the issues of money should be raised without apology or hesitation. They are an integral part of the meaning of discipleship.

Part of this first guideline has to do with honesty. Messages on money should be honest and straightforward. I have been lovingly counseled and encouraged in this regard over many years by mature Christian laity as well as by stewardship consultants. I finally know the correctness of this advice. If the need is great, say so. If the shortfall is severe, tell the people the truth. If a radical new level of cheerful giving is required, tell the people. If the pastor is struggling under the burden of inadequate church finances for any reason (as most have at some point along the way), tell the listeners how it is. Do it all with love and grace. The hearers will respond in similar fashion.

Second, the subject of money should be handled with as much humor as possible. Over the years I have carefully sought out and stored illustrations and anecdotes which allow us to laugh at ourselves, our foibles, and our reluctance to talk about money in the church. Obviously, humor is not easy to find or use properly in every situation. I continue to seek stories, and to save them with special intentionality.

Good stories, in addition to humor, are integral to good preaching. I am indebted to many friends who have shared their sermons, their sources, and lively conversations with me over the years in this regard. Speaking and preaching on the issues around money requires some honest, spirited, and relational storytelling. This book contains a fair measure of that style, and my file of such stories continues to grow.

Third, the matter of titles is important. While some preachers tend to camouflage their stewardship titles, I prefer to look for ways to bring a smile through a play on words, a new context to a familiar phrase, and other means. Here, again, only so much creativity may be possible. However, I believe that God's people will respond with a measure of genuine anticipation when the sermon title has been carefully developed. Indeed, they will look forward to the message with greater openness and less defensive posturing.

Fourth, I am committed to the best use of scripture and theological undergirding as is possible for me to muster. Today's emerging and maturing Christian needs to know the depth of concern regarding material possessions and wealth in the biblical narrative, the frequency of its mention in the teachings of Jesus and the apostles, and the many ways in which the matter of money affects the biblical witness. So many people in our churches yearn for theological integrity as to the direction in which they seek to walk on their own journey.

Nearly half of the messages in this book are taken from some precious texts in the Corinthian letters from Paul. Each time I have re-read those sections in the apostle's writing, I have found new insight and inspiration. The remaining messages are taken from other Old and New Testament texts, with some special attention to a few in the Old Testament. However, I have tried to arrange them in certain broad categories to assist the reader in his or her particular need at a given moment.

Each time I meet with a group of clergy, it seems that the issues of financial stewardship and Christian giving are high on the agenda. It is my fervent hope that this book will be genuinely useful to the church. I offer this collection for whatever use may be appropriate to the growing Christian disciple: preacher, finance committee, campaign committee, student, stewardship council, or any of a growing number of discipleship groups in any congregation. I also hope that the reading of these messages will give insight and encouragement to the individual reader searching for a deeper level of faithfulness.

Inevitably, some of the references here are peculiar to my own congregation in Bethel Park, Pennsylvania. There are a few specific references to indigenous programs or ministries, or to the calendar. I have chosen not to eliminate all of these references.

My great hope is that reflections upon the subject of money in the life of the church can be enjoyable, incisive, biblical, and relational. Giving is an essential ingredient in maturing discipleship. God grant us all the capacity to guide that maturation process wisely.

PART I
Basic Christian Formation

Some messages on Christian giving are for the sole purpose of building disciples. They may be scheduled around regular or special finance campaigns, but the primary thrust is discipleship.

One of the newest American-built automobiles carries a captivating slogan: "a different kind of car company; a different kind of car." Time will discern the truth of that advertising claim. However, the slogan captures my attention as a leader of the church and as a steward of nearly a half century of personal financial contributions to the church. Stewardship emphases need to be different in our day if they are to connect with the lives of our people.

Messages on giving need to treat persons as followers of Jesus Christ who give as an act of Christian discipleship. The church must not be about budgets or about dollars to be raised. Rather, congregations must be about growing faithful disciples. To paraphrase the apostle Paul, "The new has come; the old has passed away" (see 2 Corinthians 5:17).

One of the most affirming and encouraging comments I ever received came after my first stewardship sermon just weeks after arriving at my present church appointment. My wife overheard this comment as she sat, still rather incognito in those days, in the balcony: "Gee! That was a sermon about money that didn't feel like it was a sermon about money!"

The first message in this opening series seeks to set the tone of the book, *Right on the Money*. Giving is a personal devotion and an act of Christian discipline which cannot be avoided in the pursuit of authentic discipleship. "First Things First" reflects one of my strongest convictions about the wellspring from which giving finally comes.

"Bounty Hunt" is a message for helping a congregation reach a goal which might have otherwise seemed impossible. The specific

1

need in this instance was for about 5 percent more than we had already raised, in order to fully undergird the ministry and mission needs for the year. We had to go back to the people for a "second dip" about six months after the pledges for the year had been made. Because the message was one of Christian formation, it was unusually well received and the result was 125 percent of the announced goal.

1. Right on the Money!

"Now concerning the collection . . ." (1 Corinthians 16:1)

Someone will surely be suspicious as to the legitimacy of this text. Perhaps it is contrived or manipulated or out of context? But, of course, it is not. It is found among the most widely read writings of Paul.

Another version reads, "Now the matter about the money to be raised . . ." (TEV). Here, again, is a straightforward rendering. It is a statement which is "right on the money."

Paul takes a concern within the life of one of the churches which he had established and places that concern right in the heart of the Gospel message — which is where it belongs! Paul's statement about finances is not an isolated text. It is not an epilogue to the Gospel. It is not a separate part of the letter that was added after he was finished. It is not a postscript to the letter or an afterthought. It is not an extraneous piece of information Paul wants to share after he has presented the Gospel itself. Rather, it is found in the very heart of the Gospel proclamation.

Actually, the text seems to be sandwiched between two of the great themes of our faith. Two separate but highly relational themes dramatically surround the heart of the text itself.

An Act of Devotion

The top layer of the sandwich reflects Paul's concern for giving as an act of devotion. In essence, he writes to the people at Corinth, "Whatever you give, let it be a response to the good news that God has shared with us in Christ."

For Paul, the main thrust of that good news was very clear. He had found the matter of death to be the singularly offensive barrier to meaningful living. In his encounter with the living Christ on the Damascus road, Paul recognized that God had somehow overcome death (see Acts 9:1-9). Thus, the Gospel message was the

3

message of a Risen Lord. Death is no longer an enemy.

Paul writes in words that defy description, words which are unparalleled in their power and their poetry anywhere else in the New Testament:

> *"Listen to this secret: we shall not all die, but in an instant we shall all be changed, as quickly as the blinking of an eye, when the last trumpet sounds. For when it sounds, the dead will be raised immortal beings, and we shall all be changed. . . . But thanks be to God who gives us the victory through our Lord Jesus Christ. . . . **Now, the matter about the money to be raised**" (1 Corinthians 15:51-16:1, TEV, passim, emphasis mine).*

Do you think that arrangement is contrived? Not at all. Paul is very intentional here. And for good reason. The whole matter is a very deliberate part of Paul's central theme. When we open our hearts to the astounding message of what God has done, the miracle of sharing engulfs us!

This is the reason why, in some churches, the regular offering on Sunday morning comes as the closing act of worship. It follows the sermon, the proclamation of the good news. The offering may actually belong at that point in the service because it is our liturgical and theological response to the good news of God in Jesus Christ!

During one period of preparation for a commitment to the ensuing year's budget in my church, the campaign steering committee said, "We want to ensure that the people of this church have an opportunity to present their commitment cards as an act of worship" — hopefully, not through the mail, and not by dropping cards off at the church, and not in a home visitation, but as an act of worship. So they designed a response that year to be given as a part of congregational worship.

Over and over, we hear the stories about "first fruits" in the scriptures. God called the people of the covenant community to give the first fruits. Somehow, to give "off the top" of the pile was a more appropriate act of response to the goodness of God than to give from what was left over. Here was another symbolic reminder that giving is an act of devotion to God.

Several years ago, a friend told me a story from his own childhood. He was twelve or thirteen years of age. Across the street from his home lived a family with seven children. One day when he was playing with those children in the yard, the mother of the family invited him to stay for dinner. He knew the family to be of meager means. He also knew his presence would entail one more mouth to feed. But he decided to accept the invitation. He checked with his mother and was given permission to stay through the dinner hour.

As he sat down at the table with the family, he looked out of the corner of his eye at the window ledge just above the sink. There sat a beautiful, freshly made fruit pie. Immediately he became concerned, because he knew that his presence meant that the pie would have to be cut into even smaller pieces tonight in this large family.

The main part of the dinner was completed, and the table was cleared. The dessert plates were set out. The mother brought the pie to the table. She put the knife to it, cut a nice piece, lifted it out, put it on a plate, and set it in front of her young dinner guest. She then began to mark the remainder with the knife, dividing it equally among the others. One of the boys sitting across the table spoke up plaintively, "Mom, please don't give me the last piece of pie."

Of course, we know what the boy was thinking. The last piece of pie was going to be the least desirable piece of all, and probably the smallest. My friend said that he never forgot that symbol. The message has stood with him during the entirety of his Christian life. He remembers this event as a sign of his own giving to God as an act of devotion with first fruits.

A clergy colleague sometimes talks to his congregation about stewardship in terms of "dangerous giving." Such giving is not what comes out of the amount left over after expenses. Rather, it is giving that comes out of the same money with which we pay the utility bills, the mortgage, the car payments, and medical expenses. That kind of giving is an act of devotion.

Not long ago, I read a little book written by some denominational leaders projecting trends into the future. In a chapter on finances, they reflected on the trend of inflation and what it will mean to the church, the trend of energy consumption and attendant increasing costs, and the rapid rise in medical and hospitalization costs. I found that reading this chapter was helpful but *not central*. What we give for God's work through the church is *not* a matter of responding to trends. How we give in the context of the Christian faith is more than a matter of increasing our gift according to the inflation figures or according to the increase in the budget for the coming year. Giving is always in the felt context of the power of the gospel.

We give in the Christian life because of our awareness of the power of the good news of God in Jesus Christ. We give because of what God has done for us. We give because of the experience of the life of faith within the community we call the church.

An Act of Discipline

The top layer of my sandwich is an act of devotion. The bottom layer is an act of discipline.

With each passing year, we seem to be more lacking in the authentic discipline of life. Parents and families are afraid to discipline their children in love. They are afraid their children won't love them, or they won't respect them, or they will run away from home. Many children actually seem to be crying out for a greater discipline of love. It is a part of the God-given order of life.

We also fail to discipline ourselves in the use of our financial and other material resources. We spend ourselves to the limit and beyond. We indulge ourselves and our families in an annual Christmas buying binge, prodded by glossy pictures and enticing advertisements. We buy because our children or our grandchildren tell us that they really do "want" some specific item. We buy because the merchants' promoters tell us there will be no payments for ninety days!

Weeks after the spending binge, we sink into our chairs or sit before our checkbooks in growing depression and despair, wondering how we are going to pay for all of this undisciplined spending.

The matter of discipline is integral to the Christian life. I remember an editorial about a new phenomenon in our nation

6

known as "social depression." Most of us have at least a limited acquaintance with *personal* depression. We know how it can affect and limit our lives. A great deal is being done to try to combat such a condition in human beings. But *social* depression is different. It describes the apathy, the lethargy of a society that has lost its will and its drive for discipline.

Paul speaks directly to this matter when he says,

> *"Now, the matter about the money to be raised. You must do what I told the churches in Galatia to do. Every Sunday each of you must put aside some money in proportion to what he has earned so that there will be no need to take an offering when I come" (1 Corinthians 16:1-3, TEV).*

The guidelines are clear. Every Sunday, each one is to set aside something as a proportional gift in relation to earnings or other income.

A call to discipline is the undergirding half of this sandwiched text. The response of faith is the response of the disciplined, well-ordered life. It is not casual. It is not occasional. It is not erratic. Faith calls us to planned, intentional, structured giving. This does not negate the joy of spontaneity or creativity. However, discipline is at the heart of faithful discipleship. The Christian life is a disciplined response to the good news of God.

Paul writes elsewhere of the disciplined prayer life: "Pray without ceasing." "Pray at all times." Paul would add, "Pray even when you don't feel like praying. Pray even when it seems like God could care less about that for which you are praying." Paul calls the early Christian community (and us) to the discipline of prayer. Similarly, he calls us to disciplined giving.

The United Methodist Church is a denomination born out of the life and heart of a man who was deeply committed to the function of discipline. The early followers of Wesley were both known and ridiculed for the "method" in their Christian lifestyle. For United Methodists in our own day, and for others, such a way is still a preferred ingredient to the Christian life. It is a rich tradition within the Great Tradition of the Christian church.

Disciplined giving has several specific symbols. Offering envelopes provided and brought weekly to worship are one symbol.

They remind us of the importance of orderly, disciplined giving. Every child from about eight years of age and upwards should have his or her own set of offering envelopes — not because the church expects a great sum of money from the children, but because their own envelopes are a reminder of the life of Christian discipline at a very early age.

Tithing is a symbol of discipline. Proportionate giving is a symbol of discipline. God does not call us to random offerings or whims of giving, but to regular, systematic, proportional first fruits. Each symbol here is an instrument for growing in the Christian life. We simply must not be ashamed of our tradition or of the symbols of discipline in our traditions.

In most congregations, members annually receive a letter and a carefully composed brochure explaining the ministry and mission goals for the year ahead. Members read and reflect upon this material. But the desired response is not solely about money. Conceivably, a local church could more than meet any financial goals they had established for themselves, and *still not achieve* that which they are truly about! A congregation could double the annual church budget, yet remain in considerable darkness as to the true meaning of discipleship.

A line in one of T. S. Eliot's plays reads, "The last temptation is the greatest treason: to do the right deed for the wrong reason."[1] It is possible to do the right thing for the wrong reason in the pursuit of Christian stewardship, especially if our only action is giving money.

Engage in giving as an *act of devotion* to God and as an *act of discipline* in your own Christian life. If you grow your giving in this spirit, there will be blessings from God in your own life journey.

This kind of response is in keeping with the highest and best that we know. Even more, it is in keeping with the highest and best there is or ever will be.

2. First Things First

"But strive first for the kingdom of God and his righteousness, and all these things will be given to you as well" (Matthew 6:33).

When the church starts to talk about money, what is the first thing that comes to mind? I *hope* the first thing is *discipleship*.

I don't want you to think about budgets. There will always be a budget, to be sure. But that is not our first concern.

I don't want you to think about specific goals of specific program groups. There will be goals out there. You can count on it! But that is not our first concern.

I don't want to have you think first about your fair share of what it costs to operate the church. Surely, it does cost. You already know that.

But the first consideration must be discipleship. What does it mean to be a faithful disciple of Jesus Christ in relation to my financial resources?

Jesus said, "Strive first for the kingdom of God" (Matthew 6:33).

Jesus apparently told three dozen parables of record in his teaching ministry. Of these, about one-third were on the subject of money or possessions. Since most of the parables were about the kingdom, it can be safely presumed that this particular text is at the center of Jesus' teaching.

Jesus said, "Strive first for the kingdom of God." He then provided more stories and counsel about money and possessions than almost any other single subject. "Jesus and the kingdom" is equivalent to "Jesus and money" in many ways.

Paul picks up on this theme in his letter to the Corinthian church. He addresses the subject of offerings in that congregation. He reminds them that another church — the one in Macedonia — has given liberally and generously, even though they are in financial hard times. But Paul makes the priority in their giving crystal clear: "First they gave themselves" (2 Corinthians 8:5).

A Different Kind of "Campaign"

An effective general budget campaign for the church is truly different. It is different in part because you and I are being made different. We are being reconstructed.

In the spirit of the text, I am *not* asking the question: "What is the budget for next year?" On many other occasions, I and a host of other pastors have been hard at work trying to put together the figures of the budget goals for the next fiscal year. I have needed to know the goal toward which we are striving. I no longer have a frenzied concern for this matter in the process of teaching stewardship. I don't want to know "totals" before we make our faith promise commitments.

I no longer try to get the various program areas to submit their budgets to me early in the year. Youth ministry may be the fastest growing edge of a church's life right now. Singles ministry and music may not be far behind. What will their budget be? I may have fretted about that kind of question in the past. I no longer have a real concern about the answer to that question.

In other years, I said to program groups: "Make out your budgets, but don't expect too much. We may have to cut." Such comments remind me of something John Glenn said years ago as he orbited the earth for the first time. He was asked what he was thinking while speeding through outer space. He said, "I looked at all of those fancy instruments and gauges, and remembered that they had all been supplied by the lowest bidder!"

No longer am I carefully calculating the percentage increase in the budget. I could always guess what that percentage increase might be. But I do not try to calculate it.

There need no longer be the familiar barometer on the wall, no numbers goal toward which to strive, no red line indicating how far we have come — or haven't come, no data to give statistical encouragement (or discouragement) to the people.

The church of Jesus Christ must not be budget-driven. Rather, by the grace of God, we must be Spirit-driven. We must consider the fundamental call of the Master: "Seek first the kingdom of God."

I am absolutely convinced (after three decades of raising church budgets) that there is really no other way to run a financial stewardship campaign. We have been given a theological principle that is worthy of the church of Jesus Christ. We have a principle that is worthy in *every* local congregation.

Our goal is a spiritual goal. First things first. "Seek first the kingdom of God."

A Possible Criticism?

Some people might say that this is really the same old thing in new clothes. I understand that kind of response.

Each Halloween, my wife makes costumes for our grandchildren. She even makes some for a few of their friends. When time and material permit, she even makes one for me. Over the last few years, we have had costumes in various themes: Loony Tunes, Batman, Peter Pan, and Robin Hood. The grandchildren now have a whole wardrobe of clothes with which to play. They can interchange costumes freely.

Is that all we are really doing with our stewardship campaign — just changing the clothes around a bit? I think not. We are and must be distinctively different.

Reordered Priorities

Finance campaigns in the church of Jesus Christ shall deal with reordered priorities from this point forward.

A friend of mine tells the story of a woman who came to him in church several years ago. She said, "Pastor, I really love this time of year."

"You mean the fall colors and the crisp autumn air?" he asked.

"No, that's not what I mean at all," she said. "I mean the stewardship campaign."

"You've got to be kidding," he responded. "You actually like this time of year?"

"Yes, and I'll tell you why. This time of year makes me take stock of my life. It makes me think deeply about my priorities. It makes me ask if I am living the way God is calling me to live."[2]

That's what needs to happen to us at least once each year. We think more deeply about our priorities. Am I living in accordance with the way of the kingdom?

This is a time to center yourself anew upon the kingdom, and upon God. This is a time to put God at the center of your life once more. Stewardship is about your *faith* long before it is about your money.

We shall not just skim the surface. We will not simply go through the motions of signing a card, and then be on our way. A certain faithful pastor called on one of his members who had just come through major surgery. The man was still in the recovery room of the hospital when the pastor arrived. His pastor took his hand: "Bill, I'm here. It's your pastor."

The man came only slightly awake, looked up, flashed a sign of recognition, and said, "Oh, yes, pastor. Well, just put me down for the same amount as last year!"

Disciples ought not to just turn in a card and run. Rather, each of us must ask: "God, what is my role as your disciple right now?"

Undergirded with Prayer

The campaign must assuredly be undergirded with prayer. A worthy financial campaign will be a demonstration of the power of prayer in our lives.

Each member of a covenant discipleship group, each member of an organized prayer chain, and each member of any prayer support group in every congregation must be encouraged to pray about the consecration of members on a daily basis. This is critical to our faithfulness. Everyone is asked to pray.

A woman came home from an art sale with a framed piece of art which read, "Prayer Changes Things." She liked it so well that she hung it over the mantle of the fireplace. A few days later, she noticed that it was missing. She asked her husband, "Do you know what happened to my new art piece over the fireplace?"

"Yes," he replied. "I took it down."

"What's the matter with you?" she shot back. "Don't you believe in prayer any more?"

"Oh, yes. I do believe in prayer. I even believe that prayer changes things. I just happen to not like change!"

Some of us are like that, I suppose. We don't pray, because we sense that God might indeed change our priorities!

Let me tell you about the financial campaign of a church in

another part of the country. It is a congregation of about 500 members and an annual budget of about $100,000. Because they were growing, they needed some additional space. The space would be costly, but absolutely necessary.

The pastor organized a financial campaign committee to try to raise the money for the project. As the day of financial commitment began to draw near, he decided to send up a trial balloon. He asked the members of the steering committee to indicate anonymously on a small piece of paper what they hoped to give and to pass the pieces of paper to him.

When the total was calculated, it was quite obvious that the church was not going to even come close to the necessary goal. The pastor turned to the committee and said, "We are going to need to go to prayer about this matter!" The members of the committee may have smiled indulgently, but he was very serious.

It was just four weeks until the campaign would call for the responses of the whole congregation. "I want each of you to commit yourselves to pray *daily* for this effort," he instructed. "Furthermore, I want you to commit to one other discipline. I want you to contact two people from this congregation every day between now and commitment day, and pray with them. You may go to their homes, their place of work, or some other location. You may contact them by phone. But each of you is now asked to make that promise on behalf of this work we want to do."

When the day of commitment came in that church, the total amount pledged was more than *four times* the annual budget of that church. The people had prayed their way to an important and joyous victory.[3]

The Foundation of a Strong Church

All of this has to do with the foundation of a strong church. If there ever were gimmicks in the church, there are no gimmicks any longer.

A pastor told his organist that he was going to ask those who would give $400 or more to the special fund drive to stand at the close of the service. "Play something appropriate," he instructed.

"What should I play?" she queried.

"Play the 'Star Spangled Banner'!" came the response.

That's a gimmick. Gimmicks are uniformly inappropriate and unworthy of the gospel. The foundation of giving is in a people who are daily asking what it means to be faithful, what it means to grow and mature as disciples.

Notice the Promise!

Notice the promise in Jesus' words. "Strive first for the kingdom . . . *and all these things will be given to you as well.*" What does this mean?

It does not mean that our giving guarantees getting into heaven. It does not mean that we will have money dumped into our bank accounts if we give!

The prophet Malachi says that when we give, God will "open the windows of heaven" for us and pour down "an overflowing blessing" (3:10). And Jesus says that when we exercise a giving lifestyle, we will receive "good measure, pressed down, shaken together, running over . . ." (Luke 6:38). But neither promise has to do with winning some kind of divine lottery.

Rather, if we give, there will be enough. If we are disciples in our giving, there will always be enough. That's the unalterable promise.

No excesses are promised here — no fattened church coffers at the end of the year, no overflowing balances in our general account; rather, an abundance of *enough*. We will have enough for ourselves *and* enough for every good work. That is the promise.

Conclusion

Therefore, the church's efforts toward Christian giving are always about a whole lot more than any current financial campaign. We are not in a 100-yard dash. We are part of a cross country run that lasts a lifetime.

The church's campaign is not an effort to squeeze as much as we can out of our members in the coming year. Rather, it is a campaign to find an increasing number of persons who really decide to give out of discipleship.

Go to prayer. Don't just pray about what you will give. Pray

14

about what it means for you to be a man or a woman of the Master.

Seek first the kingdom of God in your life. Do this, and the church will do just fine, thank you. Do this, and we will have an abundance of enough for every good work.

Seek first the kingdom, and all other things will be yours as well.

3. Knowing When to Tear Up Your Pledge Card

". . . for God loves a cheerful giver" (2 Corinthians 9:7).

When I chose this title for a stewardship message a few years ago in my own church, the words set off an automatic alarm system in the heart of my financial secretary! "You're not *really* going to preach that sermon, are you?" she asked nervously. I understood her concern.

Undoubtedly, a few others thought I had gone off the deep end on this one. But the title and implied thrust of this message are both exactly what they appear to be.

The pledge card (so called) is not one of the more popular items of church life. And the time for presenting pledge cards is often looked upon as necessary drudgery among one's church obligations.

Two men were stranded on a desert island. One seemed cheerful and upbeat. The other was nervous and dispirited. The second man spoke first: "Why are you so happy? Don't you know we'll never be found? We'll both surely die on this forsaken island."

"Cheer up," replied the first man. "We'll be just fine. My church pledge is due next week, and I know the finance committee will find me!"

It is entirely likely that some church member will locate most members of any church to give them pledge cards during the appropriate season. We may even be some of those selected to do the searching for the support of a small group of Christian friends. However, I invite you to tear up your pledge card if any of several situations describe your life at the moment.

Certainly, to invite you to tear up your pledge card is fraught with some risk. Yet I candidly invite you to do just that. Here are the possible options you should consider.

First, it is probably time to tear up your card if you believe that the church no longer offers what the world needs!

If the church is simply a fine, upstanding institution in the community; if the church is simply a place where one holds membership, visits on occasion, and pays dues; if the church is in the same category as the Red Cross, the United Way, and the Heart Fund; if the church no longer offers what the world finally needs, then you should probably tear up your pledge card.

Recently, *The Christian Century* carried a guest editorial by William Willimon. Willimon serves on the Board of Trustees of Wofford College, a small United Methodist college in South Carolina. He wrote about a meeting of the Board that took place after they had hired a consultant to give some direction regarding the goals and objectives of their church-related institution. The consultant brought in his report, which boiled down to a simple statement: "The college needs to focus upon helping young people become more adult."

An older, retired United Methodist preacher who also sits on that board looked at the consultant and asked, "Sir, what exactly do you mean by 'adult'?"

The consultant straightened his back, looked at his questioner and other members of the Board, and said, "You know what an adult is. An adult is a person who is autonomous, liberated, capable of standing on his own two feet, and looking out for himself."

"That's exactly what I thought you meant," replied the preacher. "Fact is, the people in my church who believed that are in big trouble right now."[4]

The church is here because life is not easy. The church proclaims a gospel which reminds us that we are only strong when we lean on the Everlasting Arms. The church announces a gospel that tells us we are only liberated when we are free in Christ. The church reminds the world that when we look out for ourselves, we end up with a hard, crusty, costly selfishness.

A friend of mine is the pastor for a large church in Oklahoma City. The place of Sunday gathering in the building which serves that 4000-member congregation is called the "Celebration Center."

A few years ago, I asked him about that nomenclature. "Isn't that merely an attempt to be relevant, to be 'with it', to capture people's attention and imagination?"

"Not at all," my friend replied. "When we gather, we do so to celebrate the gospel. We celebrate grace, forgiveness, renewal, and the promises of God, the hope of the world, and the possibilities in Christ. The place for all of that glorious good news to be announced and repeated is our Celebration Center. We celebrate God's good news for our lives in that place."[5]

The mission of the church is fundamentally about what the world does not and cannot offer: hope, peace, strength of soul. The church proclaims a message which says that sacrifice is valued, that one finds life by losing it, and that healing means the healing of body, mind, and spirit — a holistic healing that is both temporal and eternal.

However, if you believe that the church no longer has a vision; if you think that the church no longer offers what the world finally needs, then you should probably tear up your pledge card.

A second signal is this: You should probably tear up your pledge card if giving is a chore and not a joy.

Paul says quite clearly that God loves the person who gives gladly. That statement means exactly what it says. Generally, we hear these words rendered as "God loves a cheerful giver." Such a translation is probably a bit weak compared to the actual power behind the words. God loves those who give with heartfelt gladness, rejoicing eagerly. Anything less is unworthy of Christian discipleship.

Actually, there is a parallel text in the Old Testament — an astounding verse. I only discovered it a short time ago. Here are the words from Exodus 25:2: "From all whose hearts prompt them to give you shall receive the offering for me." Both texts contain the same teaching: If you are angry or miffed or disgruntled because the church is always asking for money, then you should probably not give. In fact, you should probably tear up your pledge card.

Let me speak personally here. One of the blessings God has given my wife and me is the joy of giving. I have learned much

18

from her about this over the years of our marriage. And we both learned it as an important lesson from our families of origin.

We enjoy seeing how far God can challenge us and how far we can trust God when we make our own financial pledge to the church every year. As nearly as I can recall, every year for the past twenty-seven years we have put a number on our own pledge card that seems just a little bit beyond reason, beyond practicality, beyond the safe and possible. I do it in part because I believe God confounds our reason. God makes the wisdom of humankind appear foolish; and the foolishness of God is finally wisdom (see 1 Corinthians 1:27-28).

God makes it possible — indeed, highly probable — that we can live better on 85 percent or 90 percent of our income than we can on 100 percent. It does not make sense in human terms, but it is true.

Therefore, in our marriage, we try to make a faith promise in our giving that stretches us beyond the realm of the reasonable.

Then, incredibly, after this pledge is made, we find ourselves faced with a proliferation of special offerings for Thanksgiving, Christmas, and other Christian causes. And I say, "OK, God, how much are you going to make it possible for me to give gladly?"

One spring not long ago, we had a special offering in my church to make up the difference between our projected income and our needs for local ministry and mission. My wife and I decided to make a pledge for that offering that was beyond our financial capabilities on paper. I then earned about two-thirds of the amount rototilling vegetable and flower gardens for church members. Time restraints made the scheduling a bit hectic; but, in truth, it was great fun! If it had not been fun, I would not have done it.

Or consider a frequently occurring sequence of events. One fall, my church had a special offering envelope in the worship bulletin for Communion Sunday. The following week, the women's group asked the congregation for a "thank offering." And the next week, we received an appeal from the Council of Bishops for an emergency hunger relief appeal in a small developing country. In each case, I said, "Lord, how much will you make it possible for me to give gladly?"

In the same year as all of the above, the chancel choir began a campaign to purchase new and badly needed choir robes. My wife came to me with a bright smile on her face saying, "I think I have found a way to purchase one robe." The key was the bright smile, not the money!

Only weeks later, the music committee decided to ask the congregation to purchase new hymnals for use in worship. Time was of the essence to take advantage of pre-publication prices. Again, my good wife said to me, "I think I know a way to buy some of those new hymnals." And it was said with joy.

During all of this, the two of us were steadily working in faith to maintain our initial commitment to the regular general budget of our church.

I try to give to every appeal the church makes. (Not, however, every appeal I receive! Few of us can do that!) I cannot stand before my congregation and invite *all* of them or *some* of them or even a *few* of them to support a special effort unless I have been convinced of the need and have made some commitment of dollars myself. It is not always a great sum. Sometimes it is only a few dollars. Occasionally it can be a few hundred dollars.

However, *it must always be done gladly*. It should be fun. When it ceases to be fun, I should not do it! Giving must be a joy.

Hear again the challenge of Paul: "God loves the person who gives gladly." Listen again to the words of Moses: "From every person whose heart makes that person willing, you shall receive an offering for me [says the Lord]."

If you are not happy inside about giving to the church, for God's sake, don't give. If you don't want to give to the Communion Offering or the Thank Offering or the Bishop's Appeal or the Hunger Offering, don't do it.

If you don't have it to give, God does not expect you to give anyway. God does not expect us to give what we do not have.

For a disciple of Jesus Christ, giving is a voluntary act of the heart. Nothing less.

One Christian philosopher said a few years ago, "If we feel too much sadness in giving, if we feel torn or violated, it is better not to give." I concur.

In one of United Methodism's largest churches, the practice is to have a procession to the front altar of the church each year on financial commitment Sunday. One year, the pastor of that church wrote about the experience after it was over: "The aisles were clogged with thankful givers."

That is my dream for authentic discipleship in the church. I dream of financial undergirding for each congregation that is "clogged with thankful givers."

However . . . if giving is not *fun*, if giving is a negative experience, you should probably tear up your pledge card.

The third signal is this: You should probably tear up your pledge card when the reality of God no longer has a claim upon your life.

Sadly, the claim of God seems to be waning in our culture. More people than ever seem to *believe* in God. But more people than ever are also evidencing that such belief has little impact upon how their lives are lived. That saddens me. Frankly, it frightens me a bit.

A statistic made the rounds recently. I do not know its source or its accuracy. It said only that the average church member earns 31 percent more income now (after taxes and adjusted for inflation) than we did twenty years ago. However, the percent of income given to the church as a proportion of income has declined 8.5 percent in those same twenty years. That is a staggering statistic. Someone referred to it as "heart disease." That may be right.

Money is a positive instrument in the kingdom of God, in the reign of God. The old rabbis (including those who taught Jesus as a child) frequently quoted the mandate: "You shall love God with heart and mind and soul and strength." Then, when they explained each of those components, they said that to love God with all our strength means to love God with our "mammon" — our material wealth and all the status and power that accompany that wealth.

Consider carefully this question: Does the reality of God still claim you? Does the reality of God hold you tight? Does that reality command your attention?

As a pastor, I am the leader of a faith movement, not the manager of a charitable institution. We are disciples of the Lord of history; we are not an organization of do-gooders.

However, if God is no longer an important presence in your life, your pledge card probably should be set aside. If God is no longer even an important quest, then you should probably tear up the card.

Three Clear Signals

So, there you have it — three signals, three reasons to consider tearing up the pledge card. The best three reasons I know!

What we are finally about at pledge time is discipleship. The bottom line is not the budget total, but discipleship. The bottom line is not where we are headed, but Who is our Head!

In a personal letter a few years ago, a friend shared a story of a missionary in the African nation of Chad. He was preaching in a native church in that country, and the time came for the offering. The missionary led the prayer for the offering. He prayed passionately, fervently, and convincingly. He prayed that God would lead the people to see their offering as an expression of faithfulness, discipleship, and love for God.

In the congregation sat a woman who literally had nothing to give. When the plate finally came to her, she looked at it for a moment. Then, she slowly rose from her seat in the pew and stepped into the aisle. Quietly, she put the plate on the floor. Then, in a humble and beautiful act of devotion, she simply stepped into the plate!

When the offering plates are passed in the church Sunday after Sunday, it is not the computerized information on the envelopes that is significant. It is not the dollar amount contained within that envelope that really matters. It is the name — the representation of you and me that makes the difference.

Those envelopes are you and I standing in the plate!

Standing in the plate week after week, we need to sing with all the gusto God gives us:

> *Praise God from whom all blessings flow,*
> *Praise God all creatures here below.*
> *Praise God above ye heavenly host.*
> *Praise Father, Son, and Holy Ghost.*

4. Bounty Hunt

"The people are bringing much more than enough for doing the work that the Lord has commanded us to do" (Exodus 36:5).

One might assume that after nearly three decades of sermon preparation, this preacher would have found all the good texts about money and financial giving in the Bible. Not so! Not long ago, I came across a wonderful and amazing story from the book of Exodus. Not only had I never preached the text before, but I do not remember having read it either.

It is a story from about 3300 years ago, during a time when the Hebrew people were wandering in the desert wilderness under the leadership of Moses. After a period of time, they determined that it would be important to have a place of worship, a holy place, a sanctuary, even though they continued their wandering, nomadic lifestyle.

The story tells of the design of a tabernacle in the desert. The facility was fairly large, but also fully portable. It had a wooden frame and was bedecked with jewels, precious stones, and hangings of fine linen and other cloth. Over the wooden frame, a tent was draped. Each time the people ceased moving for a few days, they would apparently set up the tabernacle. When they moved on, it was disassembled and packed up for travel. The whole process was perhaps something like the old circus tent that moved from city to city a few generations ago.

Moses needed gifts to build the tabernacle. So a call went out: "Bring your offerings. Bring money or jewelry or precious stones or wood or fine linens. Bring whatever you can give to the building of the temple."

And the people responded. The call went out, and the offerings starting coming in.

Then, the most peculiar thing happened! There is no other known story like it anywhere in scripture. The project managers came to Moses with a request: "Tell the people to stop. We already have much more than enough to do what the Lord wants us to do. We are being inundated with offerings. Ask the people to stop bringing them."

So Moses went out among the people and said, "It is enough. Nothing more!" And the story ends with these words:

> "So the people were restrained from bringing; for what they had already brought was more than enough to do all the work" (36:6b-7).

Marvelous! Simply marvelous!

Some day before I die, I would like to preach that sermon. Some day, before I finish my journey as a church leader, I would like to hear a knock at the door from our financial secretary, who would say to me, "Preacher, tell the people to stop. We already have more than enough to do what the Lord wants us to do."

And I would stand, in turn, before the congregation and say: "Enough! There is enough. We do not have a profit. We do not have an excess. But there is enough to do what God is calling us to do."

Wouldn't that be a great day?

Unfortunately, most churches are not there yet. The church is not yet sufficiently resourced so as to stay on the cutting edge of what God is calling us to do.

So, an offering is needed. In keeping with the text for today, the offering might be called a "bounty hunt." We seek the kind of bounty that would allow the leader to stand in his/her pulpit within a rather short time span and say, "Enough! It is sufficient. We are now in a position to really do what God calls us to do."

But, back to our story in Exodus. What was the key to the success of Moses' offering for the Tabernacle? How did the people get to the point of "more than enough"? What can we learn from this story?

The Trust Level Was High

The trust level in the community of believers was high. Integrity was in place. This is a very important starting place for any offering.

There was no arm-twisting used. There were no gimmicks for keeping the coffers full. Genuine integrity was in place. There was a high trust level.

This must be true for the church as well. Recent sociological data suggest that the local church still has a strong place of confidence in the mainstream of the population, even for those who do not belong. It is terribly important that such a trust level not be eroded.

God has placed the church on a growth track. Growth is not necessarily in quantity so much as it is in quality — Christian formation, faith development, the most important kind of growth. If you take time to know the story, you will sense integrity. Integrity is very important to all of us — to the church.

Integrity was present in the desert. Therefore, the resources came in as requested.

The Capacity to Give Was Present

Who would have believed that a nomadic people wandering in the desert in the thirteenth century B.C. would have had these kinds of resources to give? They had left Egypt in a hurry. They had left so quickly that the bread had no time to rise (thus, the tradition of unleavened bread for the Passover). How much could they carry with them? But they had brought resources. Their capacity was greater than they knew, and Moses was aware of this.

The capacity of most local churches to sustain a vital, healthy ministry is clear. The church is not at the end of its rope. Unfortunately, we have told ourselves that we are poor for so long that we now believe our own prophecy! The real question is our willingness to release some of what we have for the work of the kingdom.

One of the players on the professional golf tour was heard to say, "I'm trying to arrange my life so that I die and my money runs out at about the same time. If I can just die right after lunch next Tuesday, everything should be just fine!"

The church is not in a weakened position with regard to resources. Our capacity *is* present. We are not overextended or tapped out. There is enough to do what is asked of us.

We simply need a solid offering from our God-given capacity to sustain our ministries. Some of you can give two or three thousand dollars. Some can give two or three hundred; some, perhaps, twenty or thirty; and some two or three dollars. But the capacity is present.

I believe that some of Moses' people thought of resources they had not previously considered. They rejoiced in being able to participate at a level heretofore thought not possible. I believe you might do that also.

A Free-Will Offering

This offering was also of a free-will nature. Nothing less will suffice in the ministry of the Christian church.

One church was having a congregational dinner to raise money for the needs of the coming year. As part of the entertainment, just before asking for financial pledges, a very talented senior high youth was asked to play several pieces on the piano. When he sat down to play, his first piece was Scott Joplin's ragtime number, "The Entertainer," which is the theme music from *The Sting!*

The offering in our story is not a sting. The requested offerings for the church are not a sting. They are always free-will offerings.

Those of you who are sports enthusiasts may have season tickets to one of our professional athletic teams in town. Or, if you are strongly committed to the arts, you may have season tickets to the symphony or the ballet or the opera. Perhaps you are a season ticket holder for a theatrical group. In any of these cases, you undoubtedly receive a letter each year informing you that (regrettably) the price of a season ticket is going up.

Some people might be thinking that the same thing is happening in the church. The price of a season ticket at your church is going up — or, at least, the tickets for the second half of the season.

Not so. We do not sell tickets for seats in worship in our churches. We do not have a price on a seat in Sunday school. We do not sell tickets to the divorce recovery group each week. Our ministry is funded by the free-will offerings of the people.

And it is not a matter of what you owe us. You do not "owe" the church money.

Carol Burnett tells a wonderful story about a ride she took in a taxi in New York City. She arrived at her destination and asked the amount of the fare. Upon being told, she voiced her opinion that the charges were a bit high, but then paid the cabby his fare.

As she exited the cab, her coat caught in the door. The cab drove away (fortunately, quite slowly in traffic), with Miss Burnett running along behind, shouting for the driver to stop. Finally, someone got the cabbie's attention, and he stopped his cab, got out, and apologized profusely to the actress: "Miss Burnett, I am terribly sorry. Are you all right?"

"Yes, I'm fine," she responded. And then, as only Carol Burnett would know how to do, she asked, "How much more do I owe you?"

The offering is not a matter of how much more you "owe" your church. The church is the one institution in the world that depends 100 percent upon the free-will offerings of the people. The church of Jesus Christ operates with a standard that is different from that of the "world."

The text says that the "hearts of the people were stirred." This is a vital and essential part of the process. It is the way God works. God offers a kind of "rustling" in the heart.

I recently had occasion to wear the clergy beeper system we use in my congregation for emergency contacts. Having never worn it before, I had to learn its technology. I found that it operates in two modes when a call comes in. One is to beep. The other is to vibrate. The vibrating mode is quite startling. When attached to your belt, it is a most unusual sensation — perhaps something like God stirring the heart!

Benjamin Franklin tells a story in his autobiography about a day he heard George Whitefield preach. Whitefield was trying to raise money for an orphanage. Franklin writes:

> *During the sermon I soon perceived that he intended to finish with a collection and I silently resolved that he should get nothing from me. I had in my pocket a handful of copper money, three or four silver dollars, and five pistoles in gold. As he proceeded, I began to soften and decided to give the coppers. Another stroke of his oratory made me ashamed of that, and I determined to give the*

silver. It turned out that he finished so admirably, that I emptied my pocket wholly into the collection dish, gold and all.[6]

The only way to raise money for God's work is by the free-will offerings of the people when their hearts are stirred.

What the Lord Wants Us to Do!

Perhaps the key to this whole story is in the line, "There is much more than enough to do what the Lord wants us to do." It is not what we want, but what God gives us to do. Human ambitions can be too high and too grand. This is always a danger. God's vision is what counts. We must exercise great care here.

I believe God has some significant and special visions for the people who bear Christ's name. God expects a great deal from the body of Christ right now: in youth and children's ministries, in singles' ministries (especially those who are in crisis), in training and equipping disciples for the 1990s and the twenty-first century, and some very important ministries of compassion and mercy. Jesus said that to whom much is given, much is expected. It may not be incorrect to render this saying thusly: "To whom much is given, much is *required.*"

So, we boldly ask for an offering, without apology. We openly lay it upon your hearts. We ask for a bounty, even in the desert, over a relatively short time span. We ask it in faith, so that this preacher (or any other) may stand in the pulpit in the near term and say, "Stop! You can stop now. It is enough. We now have enough to do what the Lord wants us to do."

5. The Sounds of Substance

"He sat down opposite the treasury, and watched the crowd putting money into the treasury. . . . A poor widow came and put in two small copper coins, which are worth a penny. Then he called his disciples . . ." (Mark 12:41-43).

The twelfth chapter of the Gospel of Mark records some rather strenuous debate and conflict between Jesus and Jewish leaders. The chapter begins by Jesus telling a parable about the owner of a vineyard who sent his only son to collect the crop income, and how the servants of the vineyard killed that son. The Jewish leaders very quickly recognized that Jesus was telling the story against them.

The leaders subsequently began to ask Jesus a series of questions in order to try to entrap him in some way. They asked him whether or not it was lawful to pay taxes to Caesar. They asked him some rather intricate questions about the resurrection and the nature of life in the hereafter. They asked him questions about the greatest teaching in the law.

Finally, Jesus became so frustrated by their questions and by their indignities that he turned to the people and lashed out against the scribes and the quality of their lives. He criticized their going about "in long robes," their desire to be greeted with respect in the marketplaces, and to have "the best seats in the synagogues and places of honor at banquets" (Mark 12:38-39).

The chapter then ends with a brief story of great beauty about a widow putting two coins into the temple treasury. After heated debate, intense confrontation, and great conflict, this little story becomes a climactic, simple punchline to end the chapter.

The Essence of the Story

Marks tells us that Jesus sat down opposite the temple treasury. Perhaps he sought to relax, perhaps to escape, perhaps to achieve a brief period of anonymity. The Jerusalem temple was made up of a series of rectangles that decreased in area size toward the center. The outer court was the court of the Gentiles. It was a place where anyone was welcome. The next court inward was that of the women. Further inside the temple than this particular area, the women were not allowed to go. Next, moving inward, were the courts of the men, the courts of the elders and priests, and, finally, the holy of holies. The innermost area was probably accessible only to the high priest himself.

The temple treasury was located in the court of the women. Around the perimeter of this court wall were situated a number of collection chests. Each of them was marked and designated for a particular and special aspect of the work and ministry of the temple. Such an arrangement might not be too unlike the "line items" in a church budget.

On the top of each treasury chest was a trumpet-shaped metal opening into which the coins would be placed. The coins would then spiral down the metal tube into the treasury chest.

It was in this area of the temple treasury that Jesus sat and watched the people. The one "unto whom all hearts are open, all desires are known, and from whom no secrets are hid"[7] engaged in a period of people-watching. Those who have done this in a shopping mall, airport waiting area, or other crowded place can understand how fascinating and sometimes relaxing such an experience can be.

Many people came to put money in the treasury. The Greek word actually implies that they *cast* their money in. William Barclay says they *threw* it in.[8] Such meaning is probably fairly exact in terms of what actually happened. Each of the trumpets had large openings so that contributors could place their money inside with relative ease and accuracy. They were not unlike the large baskets at some of the exit booths of our major toll highways. They are large enough so that if one is reasonably coordinated, money can be tossed into the basket from a few feet away without actually bringing the automobile to a full stop.

However, there was one notable difference in the temple treasury trumpets. They made a great clattering sound when coins were put in. The larger the coin, the louder the sound. There were times when it must have created quite a racket.

I can still remember a Sunday morning as a child in my home church when the offering was being taken. Apparently, the small piece of circular felt padding that was usually glued to the bottom of one of the brass offering plates had loosened. The usher for that day had not wanted to create a problem, so he took the felt pad out and laid it aside. However, when he began to pass the offering plates, people began to throw coins into the plates. The acoustics in that large sanctuary were such that the coins made a tremendous clattering noise. During a period of congregational snickering and giggling, the usher made a hasty trip back to the rear of the room to retrieve his felt pad and put it back in the offering plate.

By listening to the sound of the money going into the temple treasury trumpets, a skilled temple priest could tell exactly how much money each individual was contributing. Frequently, priests stationed themselves near the treasury chests in order to ascertain exactly how much money was being given.

There were many times as a child when I would travel by trolley from our home in the suburbs into the downtown section of the city. I can remember getting on the trolley with large numbers of passengers while the driver pulled a clanging chain to count the number of people. He scarcely looked at how much money was being put into the coin box. Yet, every so often he would catch people by the sleeve and remind them that they still owed another nickel or dime. I wondered how he really knew. He never even looked to see how much money was going in. However, I soon realized that it was the wisdom of experience. He had become accustomed to hearing exactly how much money made the appropriate sound in his coin box. He instinctively realized when someone had shortchanged him.

That's exactly the way it must have been with the trumpets in the temple treasury.

Mark tells us, "Many rich people put in large sums" (12:41b). Such a comment does not appear to be judgmental or critical. Mark was simply pointing out a statement of fact. There were a significant number of wealthy people in Jesus' day who were very generous to the temple.

There are wealthy people today who are similarly generous to the church.

Perhaps a few people did want to parade their wealth in some specific way. One can almost envision old Jezekiah waiting in the temple court until just the right moment to put in *his* money. He would watch carefully so that no one else was near the treasury at the same time. He would wait until an appropriate number of people had gathered and an appropriate silence was in place. Then, he would walk up to the particular chest to which he was to contribute, fling his money in, and listen proudly as it clattered down the channel. There were undoubtedly a few like him, but I doubt that such was the normative situation.

Jesus sat quietly, watching, listening, waiting. It was then that he saw her coming. Quietly, timidly, not wishing to be noticed at all, she walked into the court of the women and toward the treasury area. Mark says she was a woman who was very poor, a widow. Luke uses a word to describe her which implies that she is both poor and worn with many years of hard work.[9] With powerful simplicity and anonymity, she approaches the treasury box.

Jesus calls his disciples to him. He gathers them around him quietly. "Watch this," he counsels. Deep calls unto deep. The depth of Jesus' love and compassion and understanding of human nature calls to the depths and sensitivity in the lives of his disciples.

The woman drops two coins into the trumpet. The coins are sufficiently small so as to be worth very little. They do not even have the image of Caesar stamped upon them. As the woman walks away, Jesus turns to his disciples and says something like this: "All of these others have given out of their *abundance*. This woman has given all she had." She has given out of her *substance*. Their coins created the sounds of *abundance*. Her two small coins created the sounds of *substance*.

The Point of the Story

What is this story really about?

Some of it is simply about giving. We must not ignore that fact or gloss over it. Jesus wants us to recognize that our money is an extension of who we are and what we value in life. What we do with our resources is important. What we give is an expression of who we are. What we do with what we have left is also an expression of who we are. Jesus made it very clear: "For where your treasure is, there your heart will be also" (Matthew 6:21).

Jesus watches the people with understanding and discernment. He knows not only their monetary contributions, but also their hearts. The awesome thought that Jesus is watching each of us with that same double discernment as we give our offerings week after week is certainly humbling!

But Jesus was not a fund-raiser. This was not his mission in life. The story about the widow's gifts at the temple treasury is surely about giving; but it is a message about much more. It is a story about adventure. The more I read the New Testament, the more I realize how much of Jesus' teaching is a call to an adventurous journey of life.

Many years ago, a small-town newspaper editor asked me to give him a definition of the Christian life. He knew very little about the church, and practically nothing about the Christian gospel. I sought a word that would somehow describe the Christian life to him in language that he could understand. I finally settled upon the word *adventure*.

I suggested that the journey of the Christian life was not an easy one. It was not necessarily a smooth one. It was not necessarily prosperous. It was not always secure. But it was an adventure in living.

Isn't that what we have in this story? Is this not what was in the mind and heart of Jesus? The multitudes gave out of their abundance. What they gave would not be missed. They gave out of what was left over. They probably gave after all of their needs were already met. Some of them probably gave even after their desires had been met. Perhaps they gave as a kind of last obligation in their list of priorities. Their giving did not really cost anything. Again, Jesus would make such a statement, not to be primarily judgmental, but to set up a contrast.

The amount of the gift is not as important as the cost to the giver. Jesus is talking about risks in giving and in living. He is calling for an almost recklessly adventurous spirit.

As much as I cherish my definition of the Christian journey as that of adventure, I also know my own realistic tendency to be more "calculating" than honestly "adventurous." I am the oldest of three children. In studies of the importance of birth order in families, we are told that the oldest child is the one who is most likely to be a planner, a programmer, a calculator. Being an oldest child, I understand what that is about. By the grace of God I have sought to gradually break out of that mold in my journey of life. I am committed to the Christian life as an adventure in living and in giving. Yet, I am still learning!

C. S. Lewis records the powerful story of his almost reluctant conversion to Christianity.[10] However, once he became convinced that Jesus was the center of life, he reflected upon life with as deep a theological expression as anyone in modern literature. On one occasion, Lewis said something like this: "I do not believe one can settle how much we ought to give. I am afraid the only safe rule is to give more than we can spare."

Somewhere, there is a little graveyard beside a small country church in a tiny village. In that graveyard, the memory of a devoted soul who had spent herself recklessly and untiringly in the service of that small community is enshrined.

A brief and touching epitaph reads: "She hath done what she couldn't!" What a beautiful testimony to the faithful recklessness of spirit.

It is the spirit of adventurous living and giving that launches the dreams and visions of the church of Jesus Christ today. By the grace of God, a church hopes to accomplish what it couldn't. We enter into such an adventure by the mercy of God. And we do not lose heart.

A Final Word

There is, however, one more very important element in the story of the widow's coins. Jesus is speaking here about the importance of giving one's self. The apostle Paul talked to the Corinthian church about the importance of giving for the needs of the poor in Jerusalem. He lifted up the quality of giving in the church in Macedonia. He said of that church that they were very generous. But *first*, they gave themselves to the Lord (see 2 Corinthians 8:1-7).

As I listen to the words of this story in Mark's Gospel, and as I watch the beauty of this little story unfold, I know that it is a story about giving myself. Jesus is not after my money. Jesus is after my life! And yours!

In the quiet beauty of a momentary drama, he drives that point home: "There! Do you see that dear woman? Do you hear those two coins dropping into the chest? Those are the sounds of substance! Those are the sounds of her life!"

Most of us surely remember something of the great comedian, Jack Benny. If so, you will also remember that Jack Benny made a career out of appearing to be very tight with his money. He repeated one sketch every season, year after year, without fail. He would be standing in a dark place somewhere and would be accosted by a would-be robber. The robber would poke a gun into Benny's ribs and say, "Your money or your life."

There would be silence. The robber would say with greater forcefulness, "Your money or your life!" Again there would be silence. Finally, in exasperation, the robber would say, "Mister, did you not hear me? I said, 'Your money or your life!'" And Jack Benny would reply, "I'm thinking. I'm thinking."

Among the many stories that are told in the New Testament narrative, this is a story to make us think. This is a story of our Lord calling for our lives. Jesus calls for our lives — the ultimate sounds of substance in the plan and priority of God.

6. Good Growth Giving

"For if the eagerness is there, the gift is acceptable according to what one has . . ." (2 Corinthians 8:12).

A few years ago in the early fall, just prior to catching a plane back to Pittsburgh from Omaha, some friends took me to the Desoto Wildlife Preserve near the Nebraska/Iowa border. The preserve comprises a large body of water surrounded by several hundred acres of trees. To this spot — every year — come hundreds of thousands of snow geese on their annual migration south.

The Desoto Preserve is like a motel stopover. The huge flock of birds may stay for a few days or a few weeks — until their inner clocks tell them it is time to move on to the next station farther south. You can count on their arrival. No one ever knows the exact date, but it always happens like clockwork. It never misses.

Just like sermons on church finances! Every fall, about the same time, it happens. Congregations pause to talk about money. You can't be sure of the exact date. If you want to avoid a Sunday or two by planning elective surgery or a root canal, you never know quite when to schedule either procedure. But like clockwork, the "money" occasion never misses.

Church newsletters, messages from pulpits, and letters (usually) abound in the fall season of every year, soliciting the support of the faithful in financial promises for the coming year.

There are all kinds of approaches. The most theologically offensive to me is the one that says, "Give, and you will financially prosper!" Give $1000, and God will grant you new wealth.

The Bible does talk about the "blessings" of faithful giving. But the scriptures never promise a shopping spree.

Another approach is to encourage people to give to support the budget for the coming year. Thus, we hear comments about the dollar value of the increase, the percentage increase across the board, or the "fair share" appeal to increase income.

I don't like that approach either. I don't believe you give to the church in order to meet a budget. That's not why you bring an offering each week.

Some churches appeal to those interested in tax incentives. It's what I call the "IRS link." Give to get your charitable deduction! I resist that approach as well. I do not like to think of the church as a charitable institution.

A few will try the guilt method: "If you don't give to the church now, we may have to close our doors." Or, "If you don't raise your giving, we may have to operate only four days a week instead of seven." Or, "If you don't give, the children won't have Sunday school lessons to take home with them each week."

Guilt is a lousy trip! I don't like any of these methods, frankly.

And I don't like gimmicks. Desperate financial times in the church seem to call for desperate gimmickry.

One church tried the lottery approach. This is the approach for a society that is on a gambling roll. You bring your offering in a sealed envelope. When the plates are brought forward, the envelopes are placed in a huge circular drum. The pastor spins the drum. (Perhaps another kind of "drum roll" comes from a musical ensemble in the balcony!) An acolyte draws one envelope out of the drum and the name is read. The person to whom the envelope belongs gets "double his/her money back"!

Then there's the weight loss program. The associate pastor challenges the senior pastor to lose weight. The associate will donate $5 to the church for each pound the senior pastor loses by Christmas. It's a win - win - win situation. The associate wins, the senior pastor takes off a few pounds, and the church gets the money. Amusing, perhaps. But also sad![11]

Why do we give to the church? Why do you give? Why do you bring your offerings? Do you know?

Two ladies were worshiping at a church for the first time. The time came for the offering, and the plates were passed. The first lady reached into her purse to retrieve some money. The second said, "Oh, no. I'll get this one. You got the bus fare over here today!"

Do we know why we give?

Giving is essential to discipleship. It is a gracious imperative.

Why? What defines giving for the Christian disciple? What does true, effective, Christ-centered giving look like? Let me suggest some promising possibilities.

We Give in Order to Express Gratitude

We give thanks for what God has done in our lives. I am convinced that this is what Paul meant by a "cheerful giver." Giving reflects the wonder of grace in our daily walk. The text aptly speaks of "eagerness," giving from an eager spirit.

A friend of mine once called the pledging weekend in his church the "Glad Response Weekend." Such a description is theologically and biblically on target.

If a gift is not given in gratitude, it should probably not be given. If we feel that someone has a hook in our pocket, the gift is not appropriately given. (After a particularly emotional message on giving in a church one year, a congregation dubbed their pastor "Captain Hook"!)

We give to express gratitude and joy for the gift of life. Giving is best as "grace giving." The offering plates are not "collection" plates on Sunday morning. We give to express gratitude.

We Give in Order to Be Involved

We also give to be involved. The gift says something of what I am about. It proclaims that my church means something to me, and that I want to be involved in what the church is doing.

When I was a boy, I remember my father being frequently audited by the IRS — always for the percentage of his charitable giving to the church. Each time the audit request came, Dad would bundle up the papers and documentation, take them to the IRS office, spread them in front of the auditor, and prove his case without question. He would then tell us about that year's episode at the dinner table in the evening. It was always a very spirited, upbeat, almost triumphant conversation.

One year, however, after an audit episode, Dad came home to the evening meal hopping mad. Seldom had I seen him as angry as he was that night. He had taken the papers and cancelled checks in to the IRS office and sat down before the desk of a younger man who was probably new to the system. The auditor opened my father's records and said, "Mr. Bauknight, something is wrong here. No one gives this much of his income to the church."

Now, you did not make such a statement to my father. He stood up in front of the desk (I imagine his face was quite red), and said, "Young man, I want to see your supervisor and I want to see him now!" He took the startled agent to the office door, pounded on the door, gained entry, demanded an apology, and got it.

Why was my father so angry? Because the integrity and decision-making process in his life were called into question. He had said, "This is where I choose to be involved. This is valued at the heart of my life. This is a major part of what I am about."

We give because something in the church has caught our eye or warmed our heart or stirred our mind. We give because we have seen the radiant smile on the face of the Sunday school child racing down the hall to meet her mother after services. We give because we have been in a covenant discipleship group which has nurtured our spiritual life more than we ever thought possible. We give because we love the pipe organ that gives so much energy to worship. We give because of a sermon that set our life on a new course. We give because the church's Divorce Recovery Group has taken the broken life of a dear friend and helped make that life whole again.

We give to be involved. We give in order to unleash energies for good in the world.

This is why the time of the offering on Sunday morning is so important. It makes a statement about who we are. This is why the Bible advocates regular, systematic, weekly giving. You may choose to give only once each year. But the Bible recognizes the peculiar value of weekly or monthly giving.

Some have said we shall one day be into "auto-give" — where the contribution to the church is deducted from your account and added to the church's account by computer. I suppose we are moving gradually toward a cashless and checkless society. But I hope it does not come in the time of my pastoral ministry.[12]

We give to be involved. Each ingathering of new members in my congregation provides me with a special opportunity to hear the personal testimony of two members of my local church. I hear eight or ten testimonies each calendar year. The members share something of what their church has meant in their discipleship journey. I now look forward to those testimonies with great anticipation. I give because I want to be a part of that kind of growth.

In my congregation, we have an ever-growing number of youth involved in a multi-faceted youth ministry — in fellowship *and* in discipling. I give to be as sure as I can that these youth will graduate from high school with something secure upon which to hang their lives. I give to support an able and committed staff person in this youth focus for as long as possible.

Christians give to be involved. We give in order to bring light to what seems to be a darkening world.

A father asked his children what family gift they would like for Christmas. They told him they would like a large globe — the kind that sits on a central table and can be used for information and for imagined travel.

On Christmas morning, he noticed that they seemed a bit disappointed when they opened the globe. When he asked why, they told him they had hoped for one with a light inside.

Dutifully, he took the globe back to the store the next day and brought home one with a light on the inside. The children responded with great pleasure.

When asked by a friend what he learned from that experience, the father said, "I learned that it costs a lot more to light the world!"

Indeed it does. We know that it will cost substantially more each year just to maintain the present ministry of almost every local church. However, we give to be involved.

I have always defined "Christian perfection" as a matter of maturity. A mature Christian is one who wants to be involved, who wants to make a contribution.

We Give in Order to Grow

Finally, we give in order to grow. Some of you, upon seeing these words in the title of this message might have thought I was going to address the numerical growth of the church. Numerical growth may happen. But that is not the essence of why we give. We don't give to make the church bigger. We give in order to facilitate our own steady growth as disciples of our Lord, and to extend that same opportunity as widely as possible.

The record is clear. Generous givers are typically happier and more spiritually vigorous than those who are not generous. It has nothing to do with the size of the gift. It has to do with the level of generosity with what we happen to have. Our need to give as disciples is far greater than the need of the church for the money.

We give in order to grow our relationship with God.

In a recent book, Herb Miller reminds us that Jesus outlined three acts that relate us to God: prayer, fasting, and giving.[13] The use of money provides a real way to participate in a relationship with Jesus Christ.

A great teacher once said that the world uses people to make money while the church uses money to make people. We give in order to grow as maturing disciples of Jesus Christ.

Do you know the best definition of a "good" gift? What is a good gift for you to bring to worship on any given Sunday? What is a good gift for you to try to offer? A good gift is not a "fair share" or a "dollar increase" or a certain "percentage."

A good gift is one that has a positive effect on the spiritual life of the giver! That's the only definition that matters. It is the only definition that counts.

PART II
Toward Tithing

The subject of tithing is not easy to preach. The only healthy Christian way to approach it is as a spiritual goal. While tithing was somewhat legislated and universally expected in the Old Testament community, Jesus gave us new insight into our relationship with God which changes the Christian approach somewhat.

In most local churches, five or six new tithers per year will make a tremendous spiritual and financial difference. However, we often fumble for the right words and the right kind of invitation.

Some leaders try to invite people to approach the matter like Gideon presented the "fleece test" to God. A guest preacher in one church made this challenge one year:

> *Try [tithing] and you will see. If you have unpaid bills at the end of three months as a result of tithing, send them to me. I'll pay them.*

Another church tried a pledge card that lifted up God's "guarantee." The challenge was somewhat similar. If one had financial difficulties after three months of tithing, the church would refund the money!

I learned the importance of giving to God's work before I ever began school. I learned to tithe as a child of nine years of age with my first "earned income." I watched my parents demonstrate the joy of tithing during all my maturing years at home and beyond. I have heard the encouraging testimony of others. I have participated in the discipline and joy of tithing for all of my working life in the ministry.

Most people have a lot of questions about tithing. Isn't it mostly an "Old Testament" rule? Exactly what is a tithe? Should I look toward my gross income? my adjusted gross? my net? Why should we only think of tithing as what we bring to the church?

Is my United Way donation a part of my tithe?

Such questions need to be addressed periodically with openness and clarity. But tithing must always be seen as "gospel" and not "law." The only authentic tithe is one that is sought after or attained through prayer and devotion, and one that brings an honest joy to the giver.

I offer the following four messages as an approach toward tithing as an act of discipleship and Christian formation. I offer them as one who is still growing in his own understanding of this biblical wisdom and mystery.

7. Fit to Be Tithed

*"I do not say this as a command, but . . . in this matter
I am giving my advice. . . ."* (2 Corinthians 8:8,10).

Paul addresses these words to the early church about the
matters concerning raising money for ministry and mission. In a
marvelous piece of pastoral insight, he tells the people clearly that
he is not laying down the law, but giving advice from his heart.
His words are not at all abrasive, but pastoral and caring.

It is in this spirit that the matter of tithing should always be
addressed. Rather than "laying down the law," this subject is a
gentle, honest, and affirming opportunity for genuine growth.

Tithing is a crucial part of the legacy of our faith tradition.
Periodically, I ask myself the questions, "What is the purpose of
tithing? What is it that tithing tends to focus upon?" Let me offer
four ideas about the *focus* of tithing, all of which are in keeping
with the great tradition of our faith and are very important to me
personally.

Focusing Our Priorities

First, tithing helps us focus our priorities. It helps us ask the
question, "What takes first place in our lives?" Tithing helps us
recognize God as being closer to the very center of our being.

In the pastoral and agricultural economy of the Old Testament,
the Hebrew people were enjoined to bring not only a tithe but also
the "first fruits" of their crops or of the spring lambs to the temple
as an offering to God. It is not clear that the temple really needed
all of that produce and all of that meat as an offering. But it does
seem clear that the "first fruits" concept was an effort to remind
the people that God took first place, first priority, in their lives.

Tithing does not make one a better Christian in and of itself —
nor does the failure to tithe make one less of a Christian. But
tithing does help us focus our values. We urgently need something
to help us focus our value system these days. We are a nation

floundering for priorities. George Gallup has often suggested in his writings that America is filled with searchers and seekers after the true meaning of life. It would not alter the central thrust of his words to suggest that America is filled with searchers and seekers after *priorities* for Christian living.

Tithing helps us focus those priorities.

In our home and marriage, by mutual agreement, I handle the finances. My wife prefers not to be involved and I happen to enjoy the task. Because of my organizational and mathematical background, my system of bookkeeping consists of a large ledger where I jot down the categories and the predictable expenses in each category for each month of the year.

Several years ago, when our children were still at home, I began to realize that they were occasionally coming into my home office and looking over my shoulder when I was paying bills or balancing the checkbook. They would often make some observation or ask a question about an item in the ledger book. It was then that I became very intentional about making sure that the *first* item listed each month was the tithe to the church. The issue was not so much because I needed a reminder myself, but rather a witness to the children as to the priority system in our marriage and family. That listing has continued as the number one item in the ledger, long after those "looking over my shoulder" have moved into their adult lives.

Focusing on the Use of All Our Resources

Tithing also helps us focus attention on the use of *all* our resources. Tithing helps us focus not only on what we give, but on *all* that we spend or save.

When we take our contribution to the church seriously, it is very likely that we will take *all* our spending habits more seriously. If we take a serious look at what we give to the church, it is likely that *everything* we do with the resources available to us will be considered with deliberate intentionality.

Again, this is crucial to our time in history. We are called more than ever to be stewards of *all* we have and are. John Wesley reportedly said, "Give all you can, save all you can, and spend the rest with thanksgiving and joy." Such words are a reflection of total stewardship of all that we possess.

I am absolutely convinced that it is possible to live with great financial creativity when we tithe. I honestly believe that I can live better on 90 percent of my income than I can on 100 percent of my income. Such is not a mathematical principle I learned in the classroom or in the university, but in the school of experience of the Christian life — and I am committed to that principle.

Focusing on the Church

Tithing helps us focus on the church. It fosters closer ties to the community of believers.

This does *not* mean serving on more committees, spending more time at meetings, or spending more energy in the services and special programs of the church. It simply means that, when we tithe, we have a greater awareness and a greater involvement in what the church is all about.

Self follows money. Money is an extension of self. This was part of what Jesus meant when he said, "For where your treasure is, there your heart will be also" (Matthew 6:21).

It is part of God's plan that when we tithe, we also become more deeply involved in the organized body of believers. Significant giving yields significant involvement, which, in turn, yields significant awareness of life's meaning and the role of the church in the world.

Tithing is far more than an obligation. Rather, it is a way of supporting the church. Tithing is an affirmation of a conviction that the church is *the* God-given instrument of hope and promise for our world.

Focusing on Our Spiritual Growth

Finally, tithing helps focus upon spiritual growth. There are many tools for such growth in the Christian tradition. Tithing is one important tool.

Why? Because it involves risk. It involves trust. It involves what Kierkegaard once called "the leap of faith." There is no doubt about it. Tithing is a step of faith — especially when that step is taken for the first time, and especially when it is initiated somewhere in the mid-stream of life.

Tithing means to trust God in an unknown area. The old prophet, Malachi, makes this clear in his often cited words on tithing (see Malachi 3:10). He offers the call to tithing, and then says, ". . . Put me to the test . . . see if I will not open the windows of heaven for you and pour down for you an overflowing blessing." Malachi is enjoining us to test God and see. Tithing is a challenge to spiritual growth, a leap into the unknown and essentially non-verifiable.

If you are not a tither, I suggest you try. Reflect, discuss, dialogue with yourself, debate the issues. Test the issues and the possibilities that are contained in the promise and the call. Check out the advice of Paul and the wisdom of more than 3,000 years of Judeo-Christian tradition.

A Personal Story

As a small child I was given my first allowance when I entered grade school. That allowance was an astounding twenty-five cents per week. The instruction from my parents was clear. Five cents was to be given in Sunday school, five cents was to go into my savings bank, and fifteen cents was mine to spend.

In 1948, when I was nine years old, I began delivering the morning newspaper in Pittsburgh six days each week. After my first weekly collection from my customers, I came home with a pocket bulging with $3.50 in change. As I was counting and re-counting the money in my room — my first "earned income" — my father arrived in my room with a box of church offering envelopes. I shall never forget his words: "Son, remember that 10 percent of all that you earn belongs to God and the work of Christ's church."

A few years later, when I was a little older and stronger, I began cutting lawns to earn some extra summer money. One summer, I earned nearly $350 cutting grass. When I came home with the money, my father reminded me (gently, but firmly), "Remember, 10 percent belongs to God through the church."

During my junior year in high school, I dipped ice cream cones several nights each week and on Saturday. My take-home pay amounted to about $25 each two weeks. Once again, I was reminded and encouraged to remember the tithe.

That's all it took. I was hooked. Tithing was a permanent institution in my life. I never considered doing anything else. Today, I know no other way.

I commend it to you as a spiritual suggestion. I suggest it as a way to focus your priority system, your life in the church, and your spiritual growth. Tithing is a part of God's wisdom for the abundant living that Jesus Christ has promised.

8. Blest Be the Tithe That Binds

"Bring the full tithe into the storehouse . . ."
(Malachi 3:10).

The title of this message is not a typographical error! It does read, "Blest be the *tithe* . . ."

Encouragement toward tithing is neither a matter of law nor a matter of rules, but of grace. This, then, is a message of grace and of great promise. The title is an affirmation.

Can you set aside any prejudices you may have about tithing for a few moments? Or any prejudices you may have about "giving" in general? Or budgets? Or financial campaigns? Or even clever titles by devious preachers? Can you simply receive the text from the Old Testament in all of its power and beauty: "Bring the full tithe into the storehouse . . ."?

Blest be the tithe that binds. The key question to be asked is this: To what does the tithe bind us? I suggest four things. The tithe binds us to (1) healthful living, (2) discipleship, (3) faith, and (4) God.

Bound to Healthful Living

First, the tithe binds us to healthful living.

We need to revise a prejudice that many of us carry about the Old Testament. The Hebrew scripture is not an outdated rule book. The so-called "laws" of the Old Testament are really guidelines, God's wisdom for healthful living. They are wisdom from God to support and sustain emotionally strong lifestyles among the people of God. Such wisdom is found in the Ten Commandments (Exodus 20: 1-17) as well as in the lesser known guidelines throughout the Old Testament.

Jesus essentially took the Old Testament and put it in the context of "love." Such commands from Jesus were not new rules! When Jesus said, "I give you a new commandment, that you love one another" (John 13:34), it was not a rule; rather, it was a word of encouragement and promise for the healthiest kind of human journey.

So it is with tithing. Tithing binds us to healthful living. Tithing is a movement toward exceptional health and wholeness.

One of this century's leading psychiatrists once said, "Generous people are rarely emotionally or mentally ill." In fact, giving is one of the most profound expressions of our God-given nature. God's guidance on tithing is a call to wholesome living.

Therefore, blest be the tithe that binds!

Bound to Discipleship

Read the letters of Paul. He writes about giving, about finances, especially in the Corinthian letters (see, for example, 2 Corinthians 8-9). When we read these letters carefully, we realize that Paul is not raising money, but training disciples. He is trying to form and fashion a faithful, disciplined, resilient body of followers of Jesus. Such formation of disciples is where the church of today must clearly center itself.

A certain missionary was working to form new disciples in an African nation. As a part of his work, he tried to educate the people on the joys and the fruits of tithing, even in their simple economy. One of his special students was a twelve-year-old boy. One day the boy came to the missionary compound carrying a beautiful, freshly caught fish from the river. He laid the fish on the table with a broad smile, and said, "Preacher, here is my tithe for this week."

"That's great," replied the missionary, "but where are the other nine fish?"

With a broad smile and great excitement, the boy said, "Oh, they are still in the river. I'm going back to catch them now."

I am essentially calling, training, equipping, and encouraging members in discipleship. Tithing is a portion of that training and equipping.

Bound to Faith

Third, tithing binds us to faith. Tithing is an exciting proving ground for a growing Christian who wishes to risk stepping out in faith. It is a nurturing discipline and a sustaining influence for faithful living.

At least once each year, my wife and I try to determine what our offering will be to our church in the coming twelve months. We frequently struggle with the reality of obligations looming ahead that will require an uncertain financial undergirding: a wedding for one of our four children, one or more college tuition payments, major repairs on our home (in more than one area), and the highly volatile fluctuation of some modest stock funds. Each year, we ask: "Can we increase? Can we take a forward step? Can we move to a full tithe or beyond?"

The answer has always been the same, without exception. The answer is "yes." Tithing is a first promise to God with our resources. We both believe that when we tithe, all else in our financial obligations will fall into place. *And our faith will be stronger.*

Not long ago, I received a phone call from a member of my congregation who told me a marvelous story. She and her husband came to this city twenty-two years ago as newlyweds. He had a job. She did not. They moved into their first apartment with almost no furniture — only a card table and a few boxes upon which to sit.

They got together to work on their first budget. Her husband said, "First, 10 percent for the church."

"Oh my, not yet," she responded. "Can we get a bit of furniture first? Maybe we can tithe later."

"No, the first 10 percent belongs to God," he advised quietly.

She then recalled the story of her own reaction. "Brian, I was not ready for his insistence. But it turned out to be the best advice I ever received, and one of the best decisions we made in our young marriage. Everything has fit together financially for us over the past twenty-two years. We have control over our money that a lot of people we know do not have. Our money just seems to go farther."

Tithing binds us to faith! I do not have to remind my readers that faith is critically important in our day. Regularly, we need to be building a sustaining faith by which to live.

I heard a tragic story not long ago. It was about a nineteen-year-old young man who hanged himself. Those who found him

52

discovered a note tacked to the tree beside his body. It read, "This tree is the only thing I have found in life that has any roots."

Hundreds of thousands of people (a conservative estimate!) are searching for roots. Undoubtedly, some of you are looking for roots. Perhaps, as you read these words, you are one who is in search of a relational, durable faith.

Tithing binds us to faith. Tithing can even be a faith builder, a faith enhancer. Therefore, blest be the tithe that binds.

Bound to God

Fourth, tithing binds us to God. The spiritual connections simply run deeper.

Tithing does not make you or me a better person. The act of tithing does not make you a better Christian. We are still saved only by grace through faith. We are *not* saved by tithing, but the spiritual connections to the Eternal are more secure.

There is abundant joy and exhilaration in proving God's promises. Note that the Old Testament text suggests this very point. Part of the text was purposely omitted from the printed portion above. It reads:

> *Bring the full tithe into the storehouse . . . **and thus put me to the test**, says the Lord of hosts; **see if I will not open** the windows of heaven for you and pour down for you an overflowing blessing"* (3:10, emphasis mine).

This text does not mean that all will be rosy in our daily living. It does not mean that you will win the lottery this week. It *does* mean, however, that the connections with God will be strong and sure.

Therefore, *blest* be the tithe that binds.

Some of you may nod an inward assent in all of this. You have a knowing smile on your face as you read. Some of you identify with the deep gratitude that comes from knowing that someone started you on the road to tithing at a very young age. I know that gratitude from my own childhood.

A Place to Begin

But what if you are *not* a tither and would like to be? What if you hear the call and the promise, but you are not yet there? What if you are a long way from being a tither? What if you are secretly timid but would like to move toward a stronger tie to the rich promises of God? How do you get started?

I offer this suggestion: Set a goal for yourself that spreads out over several years. Start with a 1 percent increase in income for the next six or twelve months. Then, at appropriate intervals, take another 1 percent step up.

One of the current themes of the United Methodist Board of Discipleship in Nashville is something called "Vision 2000."[14] Such a vision tries to see where a denomination, a congregation, or an individual disciple might hope to be by the year 2000 and beyond.

What if you set a modest goal of being a full tither by the year 2000? Can you imagine the power of a congregation that seriously engaged themselves to such a goal? For every 100 households across the Christian church, this would mean an additional $20,000 per year in funding for ministry and mission.[15] Such resourcing would do far more than we can possibly imagine. The energy and love that would be released are beyond belief.

Begin the journey. God will give you validation and encouragement. The goal is worthy, and the promises are solid.

9. Tithes and Offerings

"You shall go there, bringing . . . your tithes and your donations, your votive gifts, your free-will offerings . . ." (Deuteronomy 12:5-6).

A group of clergy from a small town met every Monday morning in a coffee shop to exchange news and to relax together after the long Sunday workday. A member of one pastor's church saw the group at the same table each week and became curious. "Pastor," she asked, "why do you meet with the other pastors in town every Monday morning?"

With a twinkle in his eye, her pastor responded, "Why, we meet to swap sermons, of course."

Taking on a serious, almost parental expression, the woman said, "Well, confidentially, pastor, you shouldn't do it. You get stuck every time."

When pastors get together to "talk shop," one of the most frequent topics of conversation relates to money. Occasionally we compare church budgets. But more often, the common concern has to do with methods of raising money, teaching stewardship, and attaining the financial goals of the church program.

Some clergy truly agonize over this particular task each year. Others (although not nearly as many) thrive on it. Some, like myself, tend to see this part of the life of the church as a piece of the integrated whole. Each season is a new challenge to build more disciples.

Over the years, I have heard pastors make many unusual comments about the task of raising the next year's budget. I suppose that if I had remembered to write the comments down, they would comprise a small book. But I recently heard a comment that I had never heard before. A pastor of a larger church in our area was asking me if I was in the midst of a financial campaign. I admitted that I was. I then asked, "Are you?"

"Oh, yes," he replied. "For the next two weeks, I have to play Robin Hood in the pulpit."

I know some pastors who try to camouflage sermon titles during this time of the year so people won't know they are coming to church to hear a message about money. I prefer to work at coming up with titles that match some of the interesting texts.

I do not think it is appropriate to ask for money (or to plead for money) from the pulpit. There may be a special occasion here and there where this is valid, but not often. However, it is totally appropriate to talk about handling money and possessions in a sermon.

Did you know that sixteen out of the thirty-eight recorded parables of Jesus have to do directly with money and possessions? That is a staggering percentage when you think about it.

There are a few people who enjoy gathering statistics along these lines. I have not checked out the validity of this one, but I am told that there are 288 verses in the four Gospels having to do with money and possessions. That represents a hefty tithe of all New Testament words!

Or, here is a statistic that encompasses the scope of the entire Bible. There are just over 500 verses in the total Bible on the subject of prayer. And there are 500 or a few more on the subject of faith. But there are over 2,000 verses on the subject of money and possessions.

The message is clear. Money is a significant part of who we are, of how we live out our journey of Christian discipleship. It is important whether we are a small child with our first allowance, or a teenager with our first real job, or an adult. Money and possessions are a central issue in Christian discipleship. They are a vital part of our responsibility before God.

Look at the text for this message. Until recently, I had not even noticed it as being of any real importance. For more than twenty-five years, I have stood before congregations in worship leadership and made the following statement at some point in the service: "The ushers will now wait upon us for today's tithes and offerings." Tithes and offerings! I guess I have always assumed that this was an appropriate cliché to use. I had heard it since childhood; I heard it from my peers, so I used it as well. Unconsciously, I might have thought it was a way to give non-tithers an avenue for giving. If you didn't tithe, you could still bring an offering.

I have discovered, however, that the phrase has much more power and is much deeper than any of this. I researched the Old Testament a bit, and I uncovered the critical importance of texts such as this one from Deuteronomy. For the people of Israel, it was not a matter of tithes *or* offerings, but tithes *and* offerings. Furthermore, the offerings themselves could be separated into votive offerings and free-will offerings.

I sense some extremely relevant, contemporary implications for the local church, for the growing disciple, and for all charitable giving. To fully understand this text is to understand what it means to be faithful.

Bring Your Tithes

We are first enjoined to bring our tithes. We stumble a bit at the specificity of the direction:

> *But you shall seek the place that the Lord your God will choose out of all your tribes as his habitation to put his name there. You shall go there, bringing . . . your tithes . . ." (Deuteronomy 12:5-6).*

In short, we are to bring our tithes to our place of worship. In the older RSV, the text reads: "Thither, shall you bring. . . ." Clearly, the implications are for the church. Bring your tithes to the place of worship, to the gathering of the community of faith.

I have always believed in tithing, and I have always believed in tithing to the church. But I also realize that tithing is not a divine commandment passed down by a rigid Old Testament God to the people of the twentieth century. Our eternal destiny does not hang in the balance of our willingness (or not) to be a faithful tither to the church.

Paul chooses another term as a guideline for giving when he writes to the young churches of the first century. He calls for *proportionate giving*. We are to give in proportion to what we have earned, in proportion to what we have accumulated, in proportion to what we possess. We are to give in proportion to how we have prospered under the grace of God.

Tithing is really a symbol for planned giving. It is a symbol of a faith promise plan in our lives. A tithe is reasonably costly. When we tithe, we know that we have given significantly.

I recall a conversation with a senior high youth group about tithing some years ago. A young man was perplexed about what it meant. With a somewhat pained expression on his face, he said, "When my parents gave me an allowance of $5 a week, a tithe was only 50 cents. But now I'm earning $50 a week at my job in the drugstore. And $5 — that'll buy a whole cassette tape!"

Tithing helps us give significantly in a systematic way. It is a planned share in the purposes of God. Tithing reminds us that we are all stewards and not owners. A tithe is a guide toward responsible, healthy, significant faith promise giving.

A tithe represents what you plan to give to the ministry and mission of the church. It is your plan — freely decided upon. There is no armtwisting of any kind. It is promised out of your financial means, and cheerfully given. A tithe is the amount we bring weekly or monthly as an act of worship. To the church, each week, you shall bring your tithes.

Bring Your Votive Offerings

Next, we are enjoined to bring our offerings. The Bible knows at least two kinds of offerings which have connection with our lives today. First, there are the "votive" offerings. Votive offerings are part of a vow or promise, or they represent a specific act of thanksgiving to God, or a personal act of devotion.

In Old Testament times, the people regularly brought their tithes to the house of worship. Then, perhaps once or twice each year, they would also present a votive offering. It might be an offering of thanks for a good crop, for a financial windfall, or for an inheritance.

A votive offering might be an act of thanksgiving for deliverance from serious illness or other loss. Sometimes, the psalmist would cry out with a prayer of thanks to the God who had "lifted him out of the pit" (see, for example, Psalm 40:2). The pit was a symbol for death. What he was saying was this: "Thank you, God, for bringing me back from the brink of death itself. You have redeemed my life from the pit. And I shall present unto you a votive offering as an act of gratitude."

A votive offering might be a promise to God made in the midst of a crisis or at a time of impending crisis. Some persons degrade this kind of religious expression. They demean it as foxhole religion. I disagree. It is distinctively appropriate to pray, "O God, if you will see me through this — if you will stay with me all the way — then I will present an offering unto you." (Of course, this is a guaranteed offering, for God has promised to stay with us through any situation, no matter how severe or painful it might be!)

A few years ago, a young family was transferred to a small town on Maryland's eastern shore. They immediately joined a church there. A few weeks later, the father and the two children were involved in an automobile accident. The father and daughter were not seriously hurt. However, the four-year-old son suffered a severe concussion, was life-flighted to a special hospital, and remained in a coma for several weeks.

During those weeks, the members of their new church home rallied around the frantic, hurting family. Evening meals were delivered each day. Transportation was provided. Cars were loaned. Care was provided for the little girl so that the parents could spend maximum time at the hospital. Grandparents were shuttled to and from the airport as needed. In short, the church stayed with the family throughout the entire period.

After a few weeks, by the miracle of God's healing grace and the steadfast care of a medical staff, this child made a complete recovery. A few weeks after he returned home, the family was back in church. On that Sunday, they made a gift of twice their annual pledge to the church.[16] It was a votive offering as an act of thanksgiving and gratitude.

A special hunger offering in the Thanksgiving season could be in the category of a votive offering. We are satisfied and full. We have an abundance. Our thanksgiving votive offering in November is a response of gratitude to God.

A Christmas offering is most likely a votive offering as well. This is especially true if that offering is totally dedicated to the mission/outreach of the church.

A bequest can be a votive offering, written directly into our last will and testament. It is a way of saying, "In thanksgiving to God for all the blessings of my earthly life, I bequeath a sum of money to the mission of my church."

Bring Your Free-Will Offerings

The biblical witness also speaks of free-will offerings. Such an offering is just what it seems to be. It is an unplanned, unstructured, unexpected, out-of-pocket offering on the spur of the moment. There are few Old Testament (or any biblical) rules about the free-will offering. It is hard to make rules about something that is intended to be spontaneous!

The free-will offering is given out of a sudden impulse of love, out of felt need, out of pocket. It is the envelope in your worship bulletin when you arrive on a Sunday morning that invites a response for a specific cause. It is the call for a special disaster relief offering due to flood, tornado, or hurricane. It is the spontaneous gift to a pastor's discretionary fund for those who may be in danger of losing their homes because they are behind in mortgage payments.

On a hot weekday summer evening, just prior to a regularly scheduled healing service held each week in my church, a father and two teenage children showed up at the church door. They were a part of the wandering homeless who travel our land these days. They had literally nothing — no food, no transportation, no home, no identification, no resources, and no contacts. All they had were the tattered, smelly clothes on their backs. They had not eaten in at least twenty-four hours.

The three strangers had been drawn to the church by the sound of the carillon bells which play at 6:00 PM each evening.

One of our associate pastors was in the building when they arrived. He was on his way to lead the communion and healing service in the sanctuary that evening. He asked the three to remain in a special room until the service ended, when he could deal with their problems more directly.

Only about fourteen persons attended the service that hot summer night. Mention was made of the family waiting in another room. The pastor indicated that an offering plate was at the rear of the sanctuary for any who might like to make a contribution to their need. When the service ended, he found $85 in the plate, including one $50 bill.

Moments later, one of the worshipers returned with his credit card. "Here," he said, "use this to get them a room for the night."

Seconds later, another returned saying, "Have them wait in the building, and I'll have a hot meal here in about thirty minutes." Still another said, "I'll work right away to get some clothing for each of them to have tomorrow morning."

No one came to the service that Wednesday night to give an offering. (We don't receive an offering at that service.) But the promptings of the Holy Spirit, the compassion of the heart, and the needs of the moment generated a beautiful, a magnificent outpouring of a free-will offering.

The next morning, the clothes were at the church and ready for them to use. Money was taken from the pastor's discretionary fund to purchase three bus tickets to a small town in southern West Virginia where the father hoped to find work.

This was a free-will offering. It was the offering that said, "Whatever you are able to do, whatever you feel led to do right now, whatever you feel called to do, whatever you have to give, here is a very specific human need on our doorstep."

Bring your tithe offerings and your votive offerings and your free-will offerings to the house of worship. The text is an amazing ancient writing with a high level of contemporary relevance.

It all adds up to a single central truth: As we give of any monetary amount, we are primarily receivers and transmitters of the love of God in the world. Ultimately, that's what any giving is all about.

10. Sermon on the Amount

"Each of you must give as you have made up your mind . . ."
(2 Corinthians 9:7).

The text is very specific and clear: "Each of you must give as you have made up your mind." This is the message of genuine giving discipleship in our faith tradition. You consider your gift. You decide. You make up your mind.

However, I deeply believe that each contemporary disciple wants some advice and counsel as to what is appropriate in his or her giving. I also believe that the church should help in this regard. The church should not dictate, but help. Finally, I believe that the gospel gives us that help. The gospel nurtures a giving lifestyle.

Therefore, the question for this day is very simple: How do you make up your mind as a Christian, as a follower of Jesus Christ?

Lean into the Spirit of God

First, and primarily, we lean into the Spirit of God. This is what a growing disciple does. We pray and we listen. A short time ago, I heard a preacher say that he counsels spiritual development with his congregation along the lines of two "p's". **P**ray, and then **p**ay attention to what God seems to be saying.

Our financial process in the church is a faith development process. What we are about is *faith* raising, not *fund* raising.

A small boy wrote a note to his pastor. It read as follows:

Dear Pastor:
I'm sorry I can't leave more money in the plate on Sunday, but my father didn't give me a raise in my allowance. Could you give a sermon about a raise in my allowance. It would help the church get more money!

A true church fund drive or finance campaign is not about the church getting more *money* for its treasury. Rather, it is about more *faith*. It is about the growing edge. It is about leaning into the Spirit of God. Within this primary guideline, the Bible provides at least two other guidelines for Christian growth. Here are two principles to consider.

The Principle of Proportionality

First is the principle of proportionality. Each Christian is to give in proportion to what he or she has earned. The Bible seems to say, "Give a proportion of income, not just a dollar figure."

A man had a conversation with his pastor. He was considering what his gift to the church might be in the coming year. "Pastor," he said, "I've been considering a gift of $25 per week. Do you think that's in the ballpark?"

"What do you mean by 'ballpark'?" came the reply.

"Is my gift pretty much in the ballpark with what others are giving?" he replied.

"You're asking the wrong question," said his pastor. "The question is not whether your gift is in the ballpark in relation to others' gifts. Rather, the question is directed to God: 'God, is this gift in the ballpark for *me*?'"

Perhaps some relevant statistics will help us learn. A study was recently released giving us the "Effective Buying Income" (EBI) for the counties where I live. The EBI is that income that is available after all taxes are paid. The statistics released showed the "median" EBI for our county. The median figure means there are as many households *above* the number as there are *below*.

The median EBI for a recent year was just under $26,000.

As a result, we could say that a proportional tithe of the EBI is $2,600. Thus, if I give $2,600, I am in the ballpark for the average of a tithe in this area.

Wrong decision! Many can give much more. Many can give less. The only legitimate question is one that asks God, "What proportion of what I have do You want me to give?"

The New Testament says that the question for the growing disciple is this: "God, what proportion of what I have shall I give?"

The Principle of Tithing

There are only a few things that can be said about tithing. There are only a few sermons on tithing! I remember a cartoon that appeared shortly after the Persian Gulf War in 1991. Two church ushers are standing close together at the end of the pews while receiving the offering one Sunday morning. One usher is saying to the other, "Word has it that if the offerings don't pick up, the pastor is going to preach the mother of all tithing sermons."

I'm not sure what the "mother of all tithing sermons" would sound like. I only know that tithing is not a way to pick up the level of offerings. Tithing is a biblical tool for guidance in discipleship. Tithing is the proportional goal of a disciple.

As you may know, the Old Testament is rather hard-nosed about tithing. The prophet Malachi said that when you fail to tithe, you are actually robbing God (3:8ff). Tithing was required. Tithing was the starting point. "Offerings" were the gifts offered *after* the tithe was already in place.

In the New Testament, the picture changes slightly, but in an important way. Tithing is still assumed. It is fair to say that Jesus saw tithing as a continuing standard. The difference in the New Testament is that tithing is not a law or a rule. Rather, tithing is a spiritual discipline around the principle of proportionality. Tithing is a part of the spiritual goal toward which we move.

Football player, Barry Sanders, was signed by the Detroit Lions in 1989. He was right out of college. Many eyebrows were raised when his contract was announced at $6.1 million for five years. But the real objection came when Sanders was also given an immediate signing bonus of $2.1 million. Critics said that Barry Sanders was greedy.

Objections were somewhat silenced, however, when word leaked out that Barry Sanders had sent a check for $210,000 to his little Baptist church in Wichita, Kansas.[17]

From childhood, Barry Sanders learned the principle of tithing as a proportional gift. From childhood, he received guidance on how to "make up his mind" regarding what to give.

Or, listen to another story told to me by a pastor from another state. A faithful woman in his congregation was known to the congregation as Aunt Jane. Aunt Jane had been a member for many decades and was utterly faithful in her discipleship.

One day the phone rang in the office and the senior pastor happened to pick it up. It was Aunt Jane. "I want to talk to the financial secretary, please," she said.

"She's not in the office right now," said her pastor. "Can I help you?"

"Well, I hate to bother you with this, Pastor. But would you please give her a message. Tell her that effective immediately, my pledge to the church will go up by $1.70 per month?"

"$1.70?" said the minister. "Why $1.70?"

"Because," replied Aunt Jane, "my social security check just went up by $17 per month."

Whether you are Barry Sanders with a $2.1 million signing bonus or Aunt Jane with an extra $17.00 in your social security check, the spiritual principle of tithing still applies.

Let me tell you another story — a different kind of story. It is reportedly a true story out of the rural Midwest. A small church had just received the resignation of the church's treasurer. The nominating committee had recommended the name of a man who was the owner of the local grain elevator and a highly respected person in that congregation and community. When they asked him to serve, he said that he would under two conditions.

What were those two conditions? That no financial questions would be asked for one year; and that no financial reports would be required until the end of the year. As you can imagine, the request was somewhat difficult to swallow. But the people agreed. He *was* a highly respected man and a loyal member of the congregation.

At the end of the year, the financial report for the year was finally given. The people could hardly believe what they heard. The final payments on a long-standing indebtedness had been paid in full. All current bills were paid in full—something that was not frequently the case. All conference apportionments had been paid for the first time in at least ten years. And there was $12,000 in the bank after all commitments were paid.

"How did you do it?" the people asked.

"It was easy," came the reply. "Most of you do business with my grain elevator. I simply kept 10 percent of your sales, and gave it to the church in your name. You never missed it!"

Now, that is surely a wonderful story. But there is something wrong with the story, isn't there? What's wrong? The problem is that someone else decided what to give for the people! There's no growth in that. "Each of you must give," says Paul, "as *each of you* has made up your mind."

God wants us to grow in trust. God wants us to learn to give. God wants us to risk growth in grace through tithing. God wants us to move toward a tithe. If you are currently giving at 5 percent of income, can you increase it to 7 percent or 7 1/2 percent? If you are giving at 1 percent, can you increase to 2 percent or 3 percent, and then add 1 percent or 1/2 percent each six to eight months for the coming years?

Growth is the hope in the heart of God for you and me!

The question for each of you to ask is this: What is the next rung on the spiritual ladder for me?

My wife and I have tithed for the thirty years of our marriage. Each new financial year, we seek our growing edge. Shall we move beyond a tithe? Shall we try a new approach or a new understanding of tithing?

Tithing is not an exaction or a tax. The tithe is an act of trust, a goal of trust.

Two caterpillars were crawling along the ground when a butterfly soared over their heads. One caterpillar turned to the other and exclaimed, "You'll never catch me in one of those contraptions!"

Metamorphosis just happens to the caterpillar. There is no choice. Discipleship, on the other hand, is an act of the will. Discipleship is a move toward a higher form of freedom. We can decide; you can decide to risk becoming a giving, proportionately giving, tithing person!

There is a beautiful hymn that did not make it into our new United Methodist hymnal. It was in our 1968 hymnal, but was not included this time. I am particularly fond of the final verse:

> *To give and give, and give again,*
> *What God hath given thee;*
> *To spend thyself nor count the cost,*
> *To serve right gloriously*
> *The God who gave all worlds that are,*
> *And all that are to be.*[18]

This is the true spirit of the Christian life. This is the real joy and fulfillment of discipleship.

And this, finally, is the "sermon on the amount"!

PART III
Capital Campaigns

In the mid 1980s, my church launched a capital campaign which was to unfold over about ten years in three three-year segments, concluding with a tenth-year Jubilee. The following messages are adapted from the worship kick-off events for two phases of that ten-year effort. The first project included major changes to the sanctuary, including acoustical and energy modifications and a new pipe organ. There was an added component of 10 percent of the total for a capital need of a local church elsewhere, a part of our mission thrust.

The second phase dealt with major building changes (roof, insulation, parking, heating systems, and a special outreach ministry to older adults) which would equip us with a building ready for entry into the twenty-first century. While not specifically about money, these messages were conceived to establish vision, to build a visionary people, and to enhance a faith community and faith incentive.

As this book is written, the church is launching the final phase of this ten-year plan (albeit now extended by two or three years), and more messages on giving to build bricks and mortar for ministry and mission are being developed.

Quite often, financial campaigns for capital funds generate more controversy than those for general church ministries. This is precisely because many people do not see the vision of a building as a tool for ministry. (One possible exception might be a new or enlarged sanctuary.) Clergy, building committees, finance committees, and boards receive negative (sometimes anonymous) messages from disgruntled members.

The texts and messages which follow are pulpit offerings to lift the spirits of the body of believers, and to claim some of those who were marginal in their support.

A tonally marvelous and exciting Casavant pipe organ was installed in the sanctuary of my church during a recent summer. Some attendant sanctuary modifications were made at the same time. Structural modifications for a second building phase were successfully completed three years later. The results have been rich and marked with deep gratitude to God.

Looking back, these seem to have been the right sermons for each occasion. With a few adjustments, they are the form and text of messages which could be used for any major capital campaign.

11. Worthy Visions

"To [God] be the glory in the church and in Christ Jesus to all generations" (Ephesians 3:21).

Each week, more than twenty different church newsletters cross my desk. Each represents a different style or format for a given local church. In many instances, I know someone personally from the congregation or I am acquainted with the pastor. In some cases, the arrival of a particular newsletter is like a note from a friend.

I received one newsletter recently from a United Methodist congregation in a distant city. Among the headlines in this paper was the notice that the newsletter itself had won an award for excellence and was rated as the best church newsletter in the state. In the review, the judges remarked that this particular newsletter served more like a cheerleader than as a news and information communication sheet to the congregation.

The pastor, in turn, asked his congregation about this analogy. He asked whether or not it was appropriate for a church newsletter to be a "cheerleader."

I wonder the same thing about preaching at times. Is there a place for cheerleading in the act of preaching? Is that, in any sense, what Jesus was doing when he spoke to the multitudes in the Sermon on the Mount, saying, "You are the salt of the earth. You are the light of the world"? Is that what Paul was saying when he wrote to his beloved church in Corinth, "You are a church that is so rich in your eagerness" (2 Corinthians 8:7, paraphrase)? Or when he said to the church at Philippi, "I thank my God every time I remember you, constantly praying with joy" (Philippians 1:3)?

I suppose I do feel called to be a kind of cheerleader at times. I am a cheerleader for some worthy visions — visions that have grown out of the life and heart of the congregation over a period of years; visions that have been continuously refined and redefined, clarified and prioritized; visions that reflect "inreach" and "outreach" focal points for life together in the church; visions that usually begin and end in a great service of worship. One of the great hymns of our tradition by Albert F. Bayly includes these words:

> As we worship, grant us vision,
> Till your love's revealing light
> in its height and depth and greatness
> dawns upon our quickened sight . . .
> (THE UNITED METHODIST HYMNAL, # 581)[19]

We may have before us, at any given moment, visions that have been nurtured and grown in Sunday school classes, visions that have been cultivated by prayer and by service in the world. Such visions are ready to be set in motion for an extended period of years just ahead.

Worthy visions! But are they worthy? What makes them worthy? Perhaps we can measure any of these visions by the yardstick of a great text from the letter to the Ephesians: "To him be glory in the church and in Christ Jesus to all generations" (3:21). Under this text, what makes our visions worthy?

Worthy, If They Give Glory to God

First, they are worthy if they give glory to God. "To him be glory . . ." And how do we measure that? I am not always sure. I only know that it must be assessed time and time again.

I must faithfully make that assessment. I believe that I have an absolute responsibility before you to continuously ask, "Does what we are doing give glory to God?"

What this church does this month or this year or next year or during the next ten years must glorify God and God's purposes, or it is striving after wind; it is of no value; it is emptiness.

I must know in my heart that any such visions will glorify the God and Father of our Lord Jesus Christ. I believe that with my whole heart.

Worthy, If Faithful to the Nature of the Church

Second, the visions are worthy if they are faithful to the nature of the church. "To him be glory *in the church* . . . ," writes Paul.

Again, such a value is difficult to measure. Opinions may vary (and frequently do) as to what the purposes of God for the church really are. Every church exists for the dual mission of inreach and outreach.[20] Our "mission" is comprehensive. It includes direct involvement with hunger in far-off lands, development assistance by Christian people who care and who carry certain skills, education and training of men and women for ministry, the care of children, and the formation of Christian character and lifestyle. It includes all of these things and more.

Mission also includes reaching out to the uncommitted and apathetic thousands who live within a few miles of our buildings and who drive by this facility every day. Reliable statistics tell us that 50 percent of those who live within a few miles of any church have no formal congregational ties — and half of those persons actually *wish that they did have such ties*! Our mission is to them.

A theologically valid capital campaign that includes, for example, a new pipe organ, is based on the conviction that worship ignites the fire of faith and mission in the human heart. It is based on the notion that worship is the energizing, beginning point.

I once had a teacher who said that worship is the Christian's vital breath. The hymn writer puts it well:

> *Called from worship into service,*
> *Forth in Thy dear name we go . . .*

We are called *from* worship into the world's arena of discipleship. Our visions will be worthy only because they issue in a profound, trusting, growing reflection upon the nature of the church of Jesus Christ.

Worthy, If They Honor the Saints

Third, our visions are worthy if they honor the saints. Paul concludes his text with the phrase, ". . . to all generations, forever and ever" (Ephesians 3:21).

In recent years, "All Saints' Day" has become one of the most significant days in the Christian year to be a cheerleader for claiming our visions. What we do as a local congregation must honor the saints of the church, including every local church.

I recently received a stack of historical memorabilia from some key years in the life of my congregation. Included in the stack were nine years of newsletters without a single missing copy. (One of our saints had preserved them faithfully!) As I read, I was made very aware that those nine years were the years in which the original sanctuary of this building was dreamed about, envisioned, debated, planned, and built. The issue was not "whether" to build; nor was it "what" to build. The issue was "what kind of church" to build. What kind of church did they want to be?

Should they build for immediate and urgent need, or should they build for the ages? Should they build something cost-efficient or something highly durable? Should they build something traditional and functional, or should it be an edifice of bold architectural style and symbolism? Should it be built for present membership, or should it anticipate the future? Should it be built for a generation or for the ages?

The persistent question reflected in those newsletters was this one: Whose church is this anyway? Will what we do give glory to God? Is the vision worthy?

We are deeply indebted to the saints of decades past who visioned boldly, who steadfastly believed, and who made faith promises of financial support with considerable sacrifice.

One of those saints in the congregation thirty years ago made possible a very fine electronic organ for the sanctuary. At the time, it was the largest such organ ever built. But after thirty years of accompanying worship, that organ was dying. Repairs were no longer assured. Parts had to be fabricated from raw materials when repairs were needed. Its technology — absolutely brilliant thirty years ago — was now utterly obsolete.

What would be a worthy vision? Should we replace it with another electronic organ with a one-year warranty and a life expectancy of another twenty-five or thirty years? Or should we replace it with a pipe organ at about 50 percent more cost with a five-year warranty and a life expectancy of 75-100 years? Which is the worthy vision? Which vision honors the saints?

Shall we build an instrument for a generation, or for the ages?

In this instance, the vision is worthy because it does honor the saints. In more ways than we shall ever know, the endless line of saints leaves its footprints upon our hearts. We are a people who carry on the durability of witness in the endless line of splendor.

Shall We Cheer the Vision Onward?

I do not ask that all agree with me if that is not possible. But I do ask that you accept my convictions as real and deep for me. My convictions grow out of a deep love for the church, a love which was given to me by my parents and which has now been cultivated for nearly five decades.

I love the church. I love and believe in my own local church. And I believe we should always claim our visions if they meet these biblical criteria: (1) They glorify God, (2) they reflect the purpose and nature of the church, and (3) they honor the saints.

Somewhere I read a story about a young tourist who was vacationing in Bermuda. One day he noticed a large, noisy crowd near a pier along the shoreline. Drawing closer, he observed the subject of all the conversation and excitement. A young man was almost ready to set sail on a trip around the world in a homemade boat.

Without exception, the people along the shore were shouting pessimistic, discouraging comments to the intrepid sailor: "You'll never make it! The sun will cook you! The boat's not seaworthy! You'll go berserk with loneliness! You'll run out of food!"

Overcome with emotion and frustration, the young tourist elbowed his way to the front of the crowd, just as the little boat was drifting away from the pier to begin the voyage. Waving his arms furiously, he shouted, "You're really something, my friend! You can make it! We're with you all the way! Sail on, and God go with you!"

Sometimes the voyage of a church's capital campaign looks impossible, or poorly crafted, or ill-timed. But we are given the grace to believe that the voyage is seaworthy, and the preparations have been adequate.

I, for one, will then become a cheerleader for the vision. I stand on the shore shouting from deepfelt convictions: "The vision is worthy! The preparation has been done with care! We can make it happen! Sail on! And God go with you!"

Then, after leading the cheer, I climb down from the pulpit, jump into the boat with others, grab a set of oars, and join in rowing with all my might.

12. A Farsighted People

". . . That you may tell the next generation that this is God, our God forever and ever" (Psalm 48:13-14).

Christians are frequently considered to be very nearsighted. We only see what is up close. We never see beyond the four cozy walls of our churches, or beyond our own present life situation. Additionally, Christians are sometimes characterized as people with little or no peripheral vision. There is no breadth and no long look.

I prefer the people of God to be known for our farsightedness — always focusing on the next step ahead, always looking toward the next five to ten years, always keeping in mind the next generation!

I happen to be very nearsighted physiologically. In a recent eye exam, I was determined to be more nearsighted than ever. After receiving my new prescription, I must admit that I was disappointed. My distant vision did not seem as clear as before.

I like distant vision. I like to see the road signs ahead of me when I travel. I like to look out and see who is in the accustomed pew (and who is missing) on a Sunday morning. I like to see who is holding hands in the balcony!

I am uncomfortable with nearsightedness in the church. I want to read and study up close. I want to examine issues very close at hand. But I also want the distant horizons to be clear.

Disciples of our Lord take very seriously the "here and now." But we also take the long look. We take that long look in the spirit of the psalm text above. We are not nearsighted, but rather, far-sighted people.

As mentioned in an earlier message in this book, two friends in Nashville released a new visionary document a few years ago for The United Methodist Church. Its title is *Vision 2000* and it is a multi-year plan for the church. It focuses on leaning forward into the future. It is a way of anticipating the future with hope. I find that concept engaging and appropriate.[21]

Visions do not unfold immediately. They take time. Henri Nouwen tells of standing before a great cathedral in England a few years ago, listening to a guide outline the history of its construction. This particular cathedral was begun in 1200 and finished in 1513. Concerning that moment of awareness, he made a comment something like this: "Sort of makes you realize that one's God-given dreams do not have to be wrapped up this afternoon."

Christian people are leaning into God's future with great hope. We want to grow our own spiritual maturity. We want to equip our churches to match the possibilities of the twenty-first century. We want to claim God's visions for ourselves and for the church of Jesus Christ.

We ought always to be dreaming, always visioning new ministries, always contemplating new arenas of outreach. We need to be asking what style of worship will be used most in the year 2000, what facility needs will surface "so that the next generation will know."

I suggest several components of this visioning process.

Durability

First, our visions for the church must reflect durability. We must be sure that the place in which we tell the Story is secure.

I do not know what the twenty-first century will be like. I have had a glimpse or two. I have a few hints. But I have no certainty. I am only convinced that Christian discipleship will play a vital role.

Bill Moyers was a former aide to President Lyndon Johnson and a former minister of the Southern Baptist Church. He has received a number of awards — one for his public television series of interviews with the late Joseph Campbell.[22] Apparently, some 34 million people watched that series.

In receiving the distinguished Wilbur Award from the Religious Public Relations Counsel, Moyers suggested that religion would be the story of the next fifty years. His closing remarks at the award presentation were instructive:

I sense such a deep and powerful stirring in the world that is religious in nature, exciting, and hopeful. I am hoping my colleagues in journalism sense this and report on it because it is the story of the next fifty years.[23]

I concur. The church must be the storytelling, faith-building, discipling, outreaching, mission-launching station for Jesus Christ for all of those fifty years.

We must, therefore, make the church secure. It must be clean, dry, accessible, and cared for, ". . . so that the next generation may know. . . ."

Never lose sight of an important Old Testament notion that we begin teaching children at a very early age. The church *is* God's house. It *is* the house of the Lord. The words may sound a bit antiquated and outmoded, but they are still true. When we care for and maintain the durability of our churches, we are leaving a legacy because we are enthusiastic about the future.

Durability is our vision and our responsibility.

Versatility

A second dimension to our farsightedness is versatility. We must be ready for any form or shape of ministry that comes our way in the future. We must not "lock out" any options.

An old story tells of a man who came to his priest for confession one Saturday afternoon. "Father," he said, "I have sinned."

"Yes, my son, go on."

"Father, I stole some plywood from the lumberyard and built our dog a doghouse."

"That is indeed a mistake on your part," the priest replied. "But you obviously cannot take the lumber back now. So if you will offer a few 'Our Father' prayers, and trust the mercy of God, you will be forgiven."

There was a long pause of silence. "Well, Father, I also built a shed in my backyard."

"I see," the priest replied. "Well, that is a bit more serious. But, if you will say the 'Our Father' prayers and also seek to perform some act of Christian mercy toward another in the coming days, I believe God will forgive you."

Again, a long pause. "Father, I also built a garage onto my house."

"Now, this is getting quite serious indeed," responded the astounded priest. After a moment of pastoral reflection, he asked, "Do you know how to make a novena?"

"Father," the man replied, "if you've got the plans, I've got the plywood!"

Our mission is to be ready for any eventuality in response to the leading of God's Spirit in the years ahead. I have visited many churches which have erected new space in recent years, but with no flexibility.

If we are to be faithful to the call to erect buildings, we must be adaptable. A room used for the care of elderly Alzheimer patients during the day must be ready for use as a meeting room in the evening and a class on Sunday morning. The primary gathering places in every newly constructed building must be as accessible as possible. As stewards of the resources given to us, we must create spaces that are accessible, flexible, and durable.

Ministry Oriented

Always, the concern is for ministry. We are not a charitable institution. The church should not be considered simply another facility in the community for rent. We are not a center of business or "busyness." We are called into being and meeting in a particular building because Jesus Christ is Lord of life and history.

We are here to grow disciples. We are here to take whatever risks are required to launch ministries of compassion.

The cutting edge of creative ministry for the foreseeable future will be in the arenas of compassion. In an average size congregation of believers, it is not unthinkable to imagine one new compassionate ministry of inreach and one of outreach each new year for the next decade. In such visioning, we must pay particular attention to those who are at the edges of life — the very young and the very old.

Giving to a capital campaign in the church is a matter of funding a dream for a durable, versatile ministry. And it is carried out in the belief that God is already active in our midst.

When I was in seminary, the professors of theology talked often about something called "realized eschatology." I never quite grasped the meaning of the term until recently. *Realized eschatology* means living as if the kingdom of God is already here — in our midst. It means living as if what we dream and hope for the church and our discipleship is already true.

We need to give gifts for the construction, care, and maintenance of the meeting place of the people of God. We need to give good gifts. A good gift is a gift that has a positive effect upon the spiritual development of the giver. It is not a grudging gift. It is not an arm-twisted gift. It is not a gift given to "get these church members out of my hair." A good gift stimulates our spiritual maturity.

Many people in today's world have already decided to put their resources into other things. These "other things" are those which Jesus said are eaten by moths, and corrode and rust into oblivion. I cannot direct my resources in that direction. I am betting my life and basing my life on the certainty that the church is the most important institution we have for a sane and stable world.

Give. Give a good gift. Give so that the next generation may know that this God is our God forever and ever.

PART IV
Words of Encouragement

Pessimism periodically cycles through the church. People and churches find themselves in economic and spiritual hard times. A cartoon shows a pastor coming in the front door of his home one evening, greeting his wife with the words, "Well, it's official. The church is definitely in a recession!" A poster in the central office of a nonprofit agency in our city reads, "Due to financial constraints, the light at the end of the tunnel has been turned off."

Often, such negativism is closely linked to economic forecasts of a downturn, the "bear" loose in the stock market, or the latest statistic as to the number of persons in the unemployment line. Discouragement is contagious, and it is especially apparent in the church.

Two cowboys were riding the range one day, watching over a herd of buffalo. One cowboy said to the other: "These buffalo are the dirtiest, smelliest, ugliest creatures on the face of the earth." Whereupon, one buffalo turned to the other and said, "I thought out here we weren't supposed to hear a discouraging word!"

Negativism decimates the spiritual climate of a congregation. It puts panic in the hearts of church treasurers, and turns the courage of finance committees to jello. In too many cases, we are "poor" because we *think* we are poor!

Obviously, churches must be prudent and wise in legitimate times of economic uncertainty. Faithful stewardship is not reckless. We must be prudent and exacting in our accountability before God's people and before the world. The coming decades in the United States may well be decades of economic uncertainty.

However, we hold a faith that teaches courage and some risk. That same faith also provides the basis for such courage and risk among the people of God. The final four messages are offered to affirm that courageous stance.

13. Talent Search

"To one he gave five talents, to another two, to another one, to each according to his ability" (Matthew 25:15).

Note where the Parable of the Talents is placed in the flow of Matthew's Gospel. It is near the end of Jesus' teaching ministry. It is part of his farewell discourse. These are some of Jesus' final words, his closing thoughts on the meaning of discipleship.

The context is not too dissimilar to Paul's words in the closing part of several letters. Paul writes, "Finally, my brothers and sisters . . ." (Philippians 3:1). When Paul does write in this way, you know that he is about to tell you why he wrote the letter in the first place.

Consider, then, the Parable of the Talents. Jesus begins, "For it is as if a man (is) going on a journey . . ." (Matthew 25:14). And from there the story unfolds.

Each of Us Is Given Talents

Each of us is given talents. A "talent" in the New Testament referred to a unit of weight in money. Jesus chose to use imagery from the world of finance in this parable, but the meaning is much broader.

Each of us is given certain gifts. This is one of the principles of theology in which I most deeply believe. I never tire of reminding myself and others of this great truth. It is fundamental to the nature of being a Christian, and it is fundamental to the nature of the church.

When are the gifts given? Such a question is probably unanswerable. A Calvinist might say that they are given before we are born. Such seems to be the spirit of the Psalmist who suggests that God knows us before we are "knit . . . together in (the) womb" (Psalm 139:13).

Perhaps the gifts are given at conception. Or perhaps at baptism. Or confirmation! Perhaps they are given when we make our first conscious decision to live as disciples of Jesus Christ. If the latter is true, then God's gifts would most likely be given or begin to evidence themselves sometime between the teenage years and early adulthood.

However, the timing does not really matter. What matters is that each of us as a child of God is given talents: leadership, teaching, financial means, music, caring, listening, enthusiasm, motivation, organization, food planning, strategy planning, and visioning — the list is endless. Most important, each gift is from God. God is the source of the gifts. "[He] entrusted *his* property to them" (25:14).

Not Necessarily Equal Gifts

The parable tells us that the gifts are not necessarily given equally. We do not all possess the same gifts.

Years ago, Rosalind Russell loved to tell a wonderful story on herself. She was vacationing on a luxury cruise ship. As she sat sunning on the deck, she could not help but notice that the man next to her had a terrible cold. He was coughing and wheezing, seeming to be in considerable misery. Finally, Miss Russell offered some advice: "Sir, if you would drink lots of fluids, take a couple of aspirin, and get a good night's rest, that cold would probably be gone by morning." The man did not respond.

So she added, "Perhaps you do not know me. I'm Rosalind Russell. You know. I make movies."

"How do you do," the man responded. "I'm Charles Mayo. I run a medical clinic."

Not all of us are given the same gifts.

Each year, I meet with a group of pastors of larger churches for counsel and support. Each time we meet, I am reminded that we have differing gifts, even though we serve churches of roughly similar sizes around the country. All of us have some definitive gifts for our calling. However, we are not complete and self-contained persons in this regard. Some from the group voice a lack of administrative skills, or a lack of real ability to do meaningful hospital calling, or a seeming lack of gifts for grief work or for fund-raising. Each of us has differing, and, sometimes, unequal gifts.

When a staff person is to be replaced in my present congregation (lay or clergy), it seems very foolish for us to try to clone the person who has just left. God has given us differing gifts. No one has all the gifts, whatever "all" may mean. No one has *exactly* the same gifts as another. Each of us has gifts in differing number. Jesus acknowledges this openly. Some have five talents, some have two, and some have only one.

Churches Differ Also

Some churches have more gifts than others. Some have five talents. Some have two. Some have one. I am convinced that many churches are five-talent churches — far more than generally assumed. My present appointment is a five-talent church.

This does not mean that we are better than another church. Certainly we are not more righteous. We are simply a gifted, deeply blessed body of believers. Whether we believe it or not, most churches are!

That is why such congregations can address a number of financial issues at the same time. Some churches can build a pipe organ *and* a mission program simultaneously. Some can provide a contagiously uplifting worship service *and* expand their community mission involvement at the same time. Some can establish and fund both an active youth ministry and a strong music ministry in the same year. This is why churches can (and must) consistently take some risks of faith for the sake of the kingdom.

Many congregations can probably do whatever God calls that people to do. Because my church is a five-talent congregation, because God has given us many gifts represented in many people of many different ages and combinations, our resources and talents for the work of the kingdom are only limited by our attitude toward God's work in us.

We may put a ceiling on ourselves. We may say, "We can only go so far, and no farther." But God places no ceiling upon us. We are limited only by our vision and our faith.

A few years ago, I worshiped with a large congregation in the heart of a major city. When I arrived for Sunday school, I watched in wide-eyed wonder as hundreds of adults streamed into the limited parking places and scattered buildings for the Sunday school hour. Remember that this is not a suburban church with acres of parking; this was a church in the heart of the city, just one block from the state Capitol.

I attended one of the many adult Sunday school classes. The lesson that day was given by the chairperson of the social concerns commission. As she led the discussion, I was impressed by one comment made by a member of the class toward the end of the session: "I joined this church because I am convinced that it is a church that can really make a difference in this city."

Like that church, my present congregation is a five-talent church that can make a difference in our own city. You are probably also a member of a five-talent church! The talents may evidence themselves in a different direction, or with a different emphasis, but they are fully present. The text speaks to thousands of gathered disciples of many varying church affiliations. More Christians than know it are in a five-talent congregation.

There Appears to Be Ample Time

Note that the parable seems to tell us there is time to do what needs to be done. "After a long time the master of those slaves came . . ." (Matthew 25:19). Here, we have an interesting paradox in the teaching of Jesus. On the one hand the time is *now*. The time is *at hand* (see, for example, Mark 1:15). But in this parable, there seems to be ample time. The need is urgent. But there is time.

Growing our talents is not a rush job. It does not happen overnight. Gifts must be grown aggressively but carefully. It will take solid work on the part of many people over several years. But every local body of Christian disciples can reach its potential under the abounding grace of God. Every local congregation can worship gloriously and fellowship deeply and reach out compassionately — all at the same time.

We Cannot Sit on Our Gifts!

The only thing we cannot do is sit on our gifts. This may be the central issue of the parable. The "single-talent man" was not a bad guy. It was not that he did something wrong. It was that he did not do *anything* with his gift!

If we have the talent to help bring new life and hope to a little mission church in the city, we dare not sit on that gift. If we have the talents to provide worship that stirs the soul, that lifts the imagination, that presents the living God, and that energizes ministry and mission, we dare not sit on that talent. If we have the talent to meet an unmet need in our community, we dare not sit around and wait for someone else to meet that need.

If you have the gift of God to relate the stories of the faith to children, you cannot afford to waste that gift. If you have the financial resources to make a difference through the work of the church, if you have the marvelous "gift of giving" in your life, you dare not hold back. This is God's gift to you for you to use for God's work!

One member of my church recently said to me, "I don't know why, but God seems to have given me the ability to make money. I want to use that talent well. Will you help me?"

If we do not expand and use and invest and serve with our talents, we shrivel and die. This is Jesus' penultimate word.

If we get caught up in our own security; if we are afraid to risk; if we fail to exercise vision or to dream dreams; if we are content to stay right where we are now and move no further, then we lose it all. We atrophy. We grow stale. We wither. We fade. Jesus seems to say, "Don't let that happen. There is too much at stake. You have too much to offer. There is too much that you can do."

If We Are Faithful with Our Gifts . . .

On the other hand, if we do exercise our gifts, if we do use them to the maximum, if we *do* expand our inreach and our out-reach to the limits, then even more shall be expected of us.

How do you like that? It almost seems unfair! For those who have multiple gifts, for those who can lead and give and energize and mobilize, and for those who exercise those gifts to the fullest, even more shall be expected. What we have here is a plea for a courageous faith. It is a plea from our Lord for adventurous living. It is a plea to expand our faith's vision.

To What End?

And what is the end of it all? The promise is a beautiful one — as it always is. Jesus says, "Enter into the joy of your Master" (Matthew 25:23). Some have suggested that the word *joy* here means literally a "feast." It isn't at all uncharacteristic of Jesus to associate the promises of God with a great banquet. If you have taken some bold risks, if you have invested your talents, if you have used them well, if you have done the most possible, then share in the great banquet of the people of God.

Will you take up the challenge of a five-talent life together in Christ? Will you strengthen it and exercise it to the fullest capacity? Will you receive whatever responsibility God lays upon you? And, will you then rejoice in the greatest gift of all — the amazing, undeserved grace in the voice of the One who finally says, "Well done, . . . enter into the joy of your master."

14. Always Abounding

*"Therefore, my beloved, be . . . always abounding
in the work of the Lord . . ."* (1 Corinthians 15:58, RSV).

Every once in a while, Paul catches us offguard in the manner
in which he addresses a certain subject. Such is the case in this
text from 1 Corinthians. Paul has strategically placed a sequence
of teachings so that the flow is very carefully ordered. It is a
masterpiece of spiritual and theological truth.

First, he celebrates the resurrection faith:

> *Listen, I will tell you a mystery! We will not all die, but we
> will all be changed, in a moment, in the twinkling of an
> eye, at the last trumpet. For the trumpet will sound, and
> the dead will be raised imperishable, and we will be changed.
> . . . Thanks be to God, who gives us the victory through
> our Lord Jesus Christ (1 Corinthians 15:51, 52, 57).*

Next, he makes a general statement of response to that great
good news:

> *Therefore, my beloved, be steadfast, immovable, always
> excelling in the work of the Lord, because you know that
> in the Lord your labor is not in vain (15:58).*

Finally, he becomes very specific:

> *Now concerning the collection . . . (16:1).*

It is a masterpiece of style. And it illuminates the very heart and
soul of the giving act of a disciple through the church of Jesus Christ.

Much is being written about charitable giving these days,
partly because such giving is in some jeopardy. Some reflect upon
the revised tax laws of recent years. Negative forecasters suggest
that charitable giving will dry up in the next decade. Those who
are "non-itemizers" will benefit less from their giving. Thus, we
will see a huge drop in benevolent giving.

Other analysts reflect endlessly upon the state of the economy. Layoffs, cutbacks, underemployment, and slow growth will dramatically affect our ability and our willingness to give.

Neither scenario is definitive for a growing disciple. Christian giving is certainly not based on the tax laws. We use those laws whenever possible, but they are not the basis for determining how or what we give. Christian giving is based exclusively upon the incomparable grace of God.

There are pockets of poverty and hurt in many parts of this great nation. The geographical area in which I presently live is not immune from such changes. Yet, in spite of dire forecasts, I recently learned that my particular "depressed" area of the Northeast "rust belt" has been assessed as the second healthiest congressional legislative district in the state of Pennsylvania. Things are not always what they seem. Sometimes we are poor only because we *say* we are poor. We tell ourselves we are poor until we believe it. In truth, most of us are blessed with more than an abundance of enough.

So let us pull any conversations about giving out of the tax legislation discussions. And let us pull those same conversations out of fruitless speculation as to the state of the economy. Let us put such conversations about Christian giving into a faith context where they most truly belong.

The result is a wonderful and refreshing change of focus. That focus is upon the very act of giving itself. We do not simply write a check or pay our dues. We undergird the act of giving with drama and witness. We abound. We excel.[24]

What might it have been like to be a part of the processions to the Temple or to the tabernacle in the wilderness? What were those festive Old Testament occasions really like? Can you see each person carrying a basket of grain or vegetables, or some young lamb from the flock? Can you visualize each one moving toward the holy place with a gift in hand?

Each week, in most of our churches, a pastor says: "Let us now worship God with our tithes and offerings." That statement ought never to be taken for granted, or used as a casual cliché. There is drama and purpose behind it all.

Perhaps a small group of ushers comes forward while the people sing in great anticipation:

We give thee but thine own,
What e'er the gift may be:
All that we have is thine alone,
A trust, O Lord, from thee.
    (UNITED METHODIST BOOK OF HYMNS, #181)

Each member of the congregation touches the plates as they are passed. The ushers return to the altar, usually to the singing of the Doxology or other familiar act of praise.

In the summer community of Ocean Grove, New Jersey, dozens of ushers have been processing to the altar with the offerings of the people while the great organ plays an "ushers' march" which has been used for nearly fifty years! To some, the event may be excessive showmanship. For others, however, it is a dramatization of "abounding" in the act of Christian giving.

Some sociological forecasters indicate that we shall soon approach a cashless society. I suppose that means we will present our offering to God in a whole new manner. Can you see the instructions each Sunday as you arrive? Mastercard holders on the right! Visa holders on the left! American Express in the first six rows only! Discover cards to the balcony! The elitist "gold card" holders will have reserved seats! The word will go out from the pastor: "Let the ushers now come forward with the automated charge machines."

Giving is an act of worship. It is an act of gratitude. It is an expression of Paul's notion of "always abounding" or "always excelling" in the work of the Lord.

The text suggests not only a style, but also the amount that we choose to give. We are to "abound" in our personal decisions to give as we are able, as God has blessed us, in proportion to what we have been given.

There is a myth abroad in the culture that suggests that charitable giving comes primarily from the wealthy and from foundations and trusts. Such is simply not the case and has not been so for many decades. Most charitable giving comes from the heart and spirit of individuals and households of fairly modest means.

At least one-third of all charitable giving in the United States comes from persons who have a combined income of less than

$20,000 a year. Eighty-five percent of Christian giving comes from those whose combined household income is less than $50,000 a year. Christian giving comes mostly from people who have modest means but great faith. It comes from people who believe that life has a purpose, and who want their giving to be a part of that purpose. Christian giving is mostly quiet, mostly generous, and mostly systematic. Always abounding!

A friend and former co-worker tells the story of the "abounding" giving of his six-year-old daughter.

> *My little girl's first grade teacher lost her home and most of her possessions in an early morning fire. Our church decided to help the displaced teacher and her family through a love offering. After church, our daughter was beaming when she came up to me and announced that she wanted to give all of her money to help her teacher.*

> *I knew the child probably had only around $15.00, most of which had recently come as Christmas gifts. I felt that she really didn't need to give all her gift money away. "Why don't you give two dollars for your teacher?" I asked. But with undaunted joy, she insisted on giving everything for the teacher she dearly loved. Then, I was checked, checked from within; checked by the One who withheld nothing. And I realized that the little person entrusted to my care had suddenly become my mentor in the faith.*[25]

Let us be steadfast, immovable, and always abounding in the work of the Lord, including our offerings!

The word *abounding* actually comes to us out of the language of King James' England in the seventeenth century. It is not a word we use much today. Yet it has a rollicking, festive, expansive flair about it. It means "without limits" or "without boundaries."

Actually, *abounding* has the same meaning as *extravagance*. Extravagance can have negative implications, to be sure. If we go on a shopping spree and spend more than we intended, our extravagance can bring regrets. If we are lured into over-indulgent seasonal spending during the last month of the calendar year, we regret our extravagance in January. If we purchase a car we cannot afford, or if we purchase a vacation with a few more frills than we can manage, we regret the expenditure.

Abounding in the work of the Lord is an extravagance that has no regrets — not even one tiny regret. No second thoughts! No nagging doubts!

Abounding extravagance! This is exactly what discipleship is all about. We are continuously challenged to live lives of abounding extravagance in our prayers, our presence, our *gifts*, and our service!

Abounding extravagance! This is exactly the kind of giving spirit that will lead the church of Jesus Christ toward a new day of energy and fulfillment.

We are challenged by our faith tradition to live joyfully in the extravagance of love. And that, as Paul so clearly reminds us, includes the offering.

15. Energized Eagerness

"Now as you excel in everything [including]
utmost eagerness. . . ." (2 Corinthians 8-7).

Someone tells the story of a man who was admiring a small child in the presence of her slightly older brother. The man asked the older child, "Does she talk yet?"

"No," came the reply. "Her teeth are in, but her words haven't come in yet!"

Have you ever been around a young child who has just learned a new word? The child seems to say the word over and over. The word is savored with a special joy and used in every imaginable way.

Preachers know how to do the same thing on occasion. I once heard a sermon that was built around one powerful word from the King James Bible: *whithersoever*. The preacher used it at least fifty different ways in his message.

Occasionally, we find a word that expresses the gospel in a given moment in a very special and helpful way. We then use that word in a wide arena of spoken and written communication for a period of time.

Something like this must have happened to Paul when he wrote the second of the Corinthian letters. About two-thirds of the way through that letter, he starts to use one particular word. Before he has finished his thoughts on the subject, he has used the word nine times!

The word is *eagerness*. It can be variously translated as "earnestness" or "zeal" or "enthusiasm." However, the more precise definition (and that which is used consistently by the translators of the *Today's English Version* of the New Testament) is the word *eagerness*.

Paul does not seem to use the word very much anywhere else in all of his letters. But here he lifts it up. He plays with it. He savors it for a while. He enjoys it. And then he moves on.

At one point he uses it to pay a beautiful compliment to the Corinthian congregation. In speaking to their spirit, and that which undergirds almost every aspect of their life together, he says to them: "You are so rich . . . in your eagerness."

I cannot help but imagine how good that must have made that congregation feel. Paul, their founding parent, their chief organizer, and their spiritual guide, writes an energizing, encouraging, affirming word.

The Corinthian church had problems. No one can read these two early letters of Paul without recognizing that fact — and they knew they had problems. They knew they were not perfect, that they had fallen short in a variety of ways. They knew they had made some serious mistakes.

However, they were deeply loved by Paul, even in the face of their mistakes. It is out of this great love, out of deep respect, and out of a sure confidence in their future that Paul writes from his heart: "You are so rich . . . in your eagerness."

It is interesting to note that the text comes in the midst of a whole string of affirmations by Paul. He affirms their eagerness and excellence in faith, in speech, in knowledge, and in their love for him. What a wonderful series of caring strokes to be able to make about the people of God. You are rich in faith — a deep commitment to the realities of the gospel. You are rich in knowledge — an acquaintance with the substantive issues of faith and theology. You are rich in speech — an ability to articulate and set forth what it is you believe. You are rich in love — a strong, caring connection to your leadership, to other families, and to one another.

Paul now wants this eagerness to spill over into the area of generous financial offerings as well. He wants his congregations (and us!) to be eager to give.

It is interesting to note that the New Testament context for this writing was the economic equivalent of some "tough times." A number of the people in Corinth were very poor. Some of them had been tested by many difficulties. Resources were limited. Yet, there needed to be an eagerness to give. Paul sensed that it was there. It simply had to be drawn out of the people willingly and naturally.

94

It may be safe to say that *all* times have been difficult for the Christian church in some measure. Perhaps that is simply the nature of life in the world. Yet, in the church, there must be a continual eagerness to give and give again.

In a recent year, my church experienced one of the best years of giving in its history. The budget was tight and expenses were constantly being trimmed, but it was still one of the best years for contributions. Reports indicated that this same phenomenon was true across the country in that year. Why? Because, while there was an undertone of caution, while there was pessimism in the economy, there was an eagerness about the church of Jesus Christ.

In that same year in my congregation, we found resources among our people to restore and remodel a chapel for the congregation. That space instantly became a vital part of the total ministry of the church. Eager gifts made a significant difference.

In that same year, I found it necessary one Sunday morning to lift up the needs of a family in the congregation that was in danger of losing their home. The need was for about $1,800 over a period of six months. Within six hours, I had commitments for at least half, and within three days it was fully committed. There was an eagerness to give.

This is the spirit to which Paul speaks in this text. In spite of winds of change, in spite of uncertainty, in spite of individual setbacks, in spite of unexpected financial reversals, God seems to provide an eagerness to give. That eagerness becomes a powerful leaven in congregational life, and an impetus to the growth of individual saints.

God provides a unique and celebrative eagerness to continue, to advance, even to accelerate the work of the kingdom. God creates a kind of reverent impatience among us. And we give as a movement of the Spirit.

A resident of Maine recently told of his little hometown that was deliberately flooded as a part of the Army Corps of Engineers project to build a sizeable dam. The man said that the most painful part of that experience (besides the relocation) was watching his town die. He said that all improvements and repairs ceased. Why paint a house that was soon to be covered with water? Why repair a building when the whole town was to be wiped out?

Why worry about rubbish and potholes in the streets or graffiti on the walls? Week after week, the whole town became more bedraggled and run down.

The sad truth is this: When there is no faith in the future, there is no power in the present!

God has given you and me a sure and certain faith in the future. The fruits of that faith are a rich eagerness to finish the course, to dream boldly, and to keep the faith.

When our own children were teenagers, we were obliged to listen to a national disc jockey chart the weekly countdown of the top forty songs in the nation on our car or home radio on Sunday afternoons. Just before this man would sign off the air each Sunday afternoon, he would say: "Remember! Keep your feet on the ground and reach for the stars."

That's the kind of eagerness that is needed among us in our Christian formation: to keep our feet on the ground and reach for the stars. We must maintain a certain degree of wisdom and commonsense about the realities with which we live, and then reach for the very best toward which God calls us.

Finally, we should note that Paul concludes his message to the Corinthian church with a very important, insightful, and useful statement: "Your eagerness has stirred up most of [the others]" (2 Corinthians 9:2, TEV).

Eagerness generates eagerness. It can become a positive addiction for disciples. The dynamism of eagerness is highly contagious.

Let your eagerness and energy for a thoughtful faith, for creativity, and for loving community be carefully linked to your eagerness to give generously. Such eager energy will strengthen the whole of your discipleship journey.

16. Possibilities in the Midst of Leanness

"To [God] who . . . is able to accomplish abundantly far more than all we can ask or imagine, to him be the glory in the church and in Christ Jesus . . ." (Ephesians 3:20-21).

Over the years of my ministry, my wife and I have had the privilege of leading a number of marriage retreats. One of the strategies we have used to begin introducing couples to one another in the early hours of such retreats is an exercise my wife calls "able words." Each member of the group is asked to list a number of "able words" for his or her spouse.

Immediately, some traditional kinds of words come to mind and are suggested: capable, lovable, huggable, amiable, sociable, reliable.

However, we have frequently challenged the couples to be inventive with their words, to create some words that are uniquely their own. To prime the pump a bit, she suggests that I am one who is organize-able or schedule-able or structure-able. And I respond that she is definitely spontaneous-able.

She says that I like to eat, so I am eat-able. I retort that she is eat-out-able! She may say that I am preach-able. And I respond that she is listen-able.

And so it goes. The process takes wings amidst laughter and abundant conversation. We find new and affirming able words to describe one another.

In a similar fashion, the apostle Paul uses some "able" words to describe the nature of God:

> *"Now to God who is **able** to strengthen you . . ."*
> *(Romans 16:25).*

Or:

> *"God is **able** to provide you with every blessing in abundance" (2 Corinthians 9:8).*

Or, in a kind of reverse psychology:

> *Nothing "will be **able** to separate us from the love of God."*
> *(Romans 8:39).*

Or, finally, in the text for this message:

> *God "is **able** to accomplish abundantly far more than all*
> *we can ask or imagine . . ." (Ephesians 3:20).*

The Ephesians text is a great doxology of New Testament praise, following one of the greatest theological expressions in prayer ever written. Some say that it is a spontaneous ecstatic utterance of Paul, caught up in the joy of faith. Others say that the passage is a part of the hymnody and liturgy of the early church. Whatever is the case, we have a priceless fragment of scripture worthy of memorization, worthy of being written permanently on the tablets of our hearts. It is directed to believers in the church in a very specific way.

"God is able. . . ." Here is one of the most dramatic, descriptive, dynamic, directed "able" words of all. It focuses upon the heart of faith — a faith rooted in God, revealed in Jesus Christ, and set in motion through the church.

We need this text today. It is written for us. It is written for those in the church who are burdened with doubt, discouragement, despair, hard times, and by a sense of powerlessness. It is written for those in the church who feel hopeless about the call to change the world around us. It is written for those in the church who still hold God close to their hearts, but who have no sense that God can make any real difference in the world outside the four walls. It is written for those who believe that the times are too lean for definitive action, and they can play no definitive part in that action.

We are occasionally afflicted by a sense of leanness in our discipleship. (Sometimes the affliction is chronic!) We lack confidence that anything significant can really happen, or that we can participate meaningfully in a viable, life-changing ministry.

Our text is a word of possibility in the midst of the leanness of our times. God is able!

Southwestern Pennsylvania has experienced a certain "leanness" mentality in recent years. Personally, I love this section of our nation. I grew up in Pittsburgh. I have a great fondness for this part of our land.

But I have heard many words of despair and discouragement: We are the "rust belt" of the nation. Industry is leaving, never to return. Our base population of young people is being depleted. We are in for hard times ahead.

Hardship and uncertainty prevail. Christians are not sure how to respond. Some have helped with food banks and other emergency agencies. Others have reacted with anger and frustration. A few have exercised some tactics of confrontation that are inappropriate and unworthy of the people of God, even if one understands the depth of emotion from which those tactics come.

The dominant response, however, has been to crawl into a shell, take care of ourselves as best we can, and hope for the best — including any forgiveness from God for neglected ministries of discipling and compassion.

What if we took our text seriously? What if the church became an instrument of hope and possibility in a time of some economic leanness? What if confident disciples took the initiative to call upon the corporate, economic, business, and educational leaders of our area for serious reflection and strategic planning? What if community leaders of Christian persuasion met under the umbrella of prayer and the light of this text? What if we trusted this text?

We would not try to reclaim what is gone. Rather, we would explore new possibilities within our natural and human resources.

God is able, through God's people, to do far more abundantly than we even dream! There are distinct possibilities in the midst of leanness.

The mentality of a regional or national economic recession affects the mentality (and, frequently, the spirituality) of the church. We spend a great deal of time worrying about corporate restructuring and re-positioning of persons, and how those factors will affect the church budget. We worry about the financial implications of early retirement. The leadership structure of a church becomes unsettled in such times.

There is a wonderful story about a group of people gathering to watch the display of great strength by a powerfully built man. His presentation consisted of taking a fresh orange and squeezing it in one hand until the fruit was reduced to dry pulp. He would then challenge anyone in the audience to obtain any more liquid from the pulp.

On one occasion, a frail, older man, slightly built, stepped forward and said that he would like to accept the challenge. The strong man smiled, but felt he must indulge this old-timer. The older man stepped onto the platform, took the orange pulp, and began to squeeze. The crowd watched in silence and skepticism. However, within a few minutes, two or three drops of juice came through the older man's hands and fell to the ground.

"That's amazing," said the strong man. "No one has ever been able to do that before. How did you do it?"

"It was easy," came the reply. "You see, I'm the treasurer of my local church."

Leaner times bring out stories like that one. Church giving and church budgets are like getting juice from a pulp that is already squeezed dry.

Does this mean we should not plan and dream for the future? Does it mean that it is impossible for us to match or exceed the dreams of those who saw possibilities for the mission and ministry of our congregations of an earlier generation, those who dared to adventure in their own lean times? Does all of this mean that we should not risk a plan, a strategy for mission and ministry into the twenty-first century? Of course not!

Ours is a faith that affirms possibilities in the midst of leanness. We do not affirm them naively, or irresponsibly, or in accordance with some humanistic scheme. We do it because *God is able. . . through the church . . . to do so much more*!

The translators of the New Testament must have had a difficult time with some of the texts in this particular passage in Ephesians. The RSV reads: "God is able to do *far more abundantly*." J. B. Phillips, in a careful paraphrase, reads: "God is able to do *infinitely more*." The New English Bible tries yet another approach: "God is able to do *immeasurably more*."

I found it fascinating, however, to go back to the old King James rendering of 1611. Here, we read, "God is able to do *exceeding abundantly*." Marvelous! What a beautiful overstatement! God is able to do exceeding abundantly above all we ask or think!

That is the spirit of Christian discipleship and adventure.

J. B. Phillips wrote a little book many years ago whose title is still descriptive for the church: *Your God Is Too Small*.[26] Such a phenomenon is still a central problem for God's people.

Yet, God is still able to do exceeding abundantly above all we ask or think through you and me, and in Jesus Christ!

I look back today and thank God for all the saints who knew the power of this verse. I thank God for all the saints in the congregations I have known in my lifetime — including those of my childhood. I thank God especially for the saints in the life and history of my current church who set dreams in motion over past decades. I thank God for saints who know how to dream today, even in times of leanness, hardship, and uncertainty.

I look at myself. I look at all of us. I think of the saints who have marked the way for me in the church of Jesus Christ. And I know there is much more yet to be revealed.

You and I can believe this text. It is a word to be trusted. It is a place to stand. God is able to do far more abundantly than all we ask or think, by the power at work in us.

It is not our own doing. We do not earn it or deserve it. It is an act of grace. It is a gift of grace.

God is able to do more than we can dream.

We have a vision of possibilities in the midst of leanness. Let us take hold of that vision with joy, and exercise it with confidence and great thanksgiving.

Endnotes

[1]"Murder in the Cathedral," as published in *T. S. Eliot: The Complete Poems and Plays, 1909-1950* (New York: Harcourt, Brace, and Company, 1952), p. 196.

[2]From Norman Neaves, *Church of the Servant* (Oklahoma City). Used by permission.

[3]The Goodrich United Methodist Church, Norman, Oklahoma, Rev. Jim Ramsey, Pastor. Recounted by Norman Neaves on May 26, 1991.

[4]*The Christian Century*, Vol. 105, No. 26 (September 14-21, 1988), p. 790.

[5]From a conversation with Dr. Norman Neaves, Church of the Servant (United Methodist), Oklahoma City, Oklahoma.

[6]Benjamin Franklin, *The Autobiography of Benjamin Franklin* (New Haven: Yale University Press, 1964), p. 177.

[7]From the "Prayer of Confession" in *The Book of Worship for Church and Home* (Nashville: United Methodist Publishing House, 1965), p. 16.

[8]William Barclay's translation as found in *The Gospel of Mark*, in *The Daily Study Bible* (Philadelphia: Westminster Press, 1956), p. 315.

[9]*The Interpreter's Bible*, Volume VIII (New York: Abingdon Press, 1952), p. 359.

[10]See his autobiography, *Surprised by Joy: The Shape of My Early Life*, (New York: Harcourt, Brace & World, Inc., 1955).

[11]The last two "gimmicks" are suggested by Ernest T. Campbell in *Campbell's Notebook: A Quarterly for Those Who Preach*, October 1989 (P.O. Box 7, New York, NY 10033).

[12]Early in 1990, I received a newsletter from a church in another part of the country which had introduced "Auto-give" in their giving plan for the coming year. I do not fault their decision. I do, however, hope that I never have to make the decision to introduce such patterns into the life of my congregation.

[13]Herb Miller, *The Vital Congregation* (Nashville: Abingdon, 1990), pp. 113-14.

[14]Joe A. Harding and Ralph W. Mohney, *Vision 2000: Planning for Ministry into the Next Century* (Nashville: Discipleship Resources, 1991).

[15]Based on an estimated household income of $20,000, moving from 2 percent of income given in year #1 and 3 percent of income given in year #2. The same 100 households who were giving $40,000 in 1992 would be giving $200,000 in 2000, assuming no increase in household income.

[16]As told in 1984 by Rev. Errol Smith, while pastor of Faith United Methodist Church, Rockville, Maryland. Used by permission.

[17]Austin Murphy, "A Lamb Among Lions," *Sports Illustrated*, Vol. 73 (Sept. 10, 1990), p. 60.

[18]From G. A. Studdert-Kennedy, "Awake, Awake to Love and Work" (Kent, England: Hodder & Stoughton Publishers).

[19]By Albert F. Bayly (1901-84). Copyright © 1961. Reprinted by permission of Oxford University Press.

[20]These are terms I have used for many years to designate the balanced life of any local congregation. *Inreach* has to do with the development of the spirit and Christian formation. *Outreach* has to do with a compassionate, merciful, and just ministry in the community and the world.

[21]Joe Harding and Ralph Mohney, *Vision 2000*.

[22]Published under the title, *Joseph Campbell: The Power of Myth*, with Bill Moyers (New York: Doubleday, 1988).

[23]From a news report cited by the Rev. Rodney Wilmoth, St. Paul United Methodist Church, Omaha, Nebraska.

[24]This particular message uses *both* the RSV and NRSV renderings of the text. *Abounding* is the word in the RSV. *Excelling* is in the NRSV. Both are words alive with meaning and possibility for the Christian journey.

[25]As told by the Rev. Stephen L. Martyn in the newsletter of the Idalou United Methodist Church, Idalou, Texas, in the winter of 1988. Used by permission.

[26]William Barclay, *Your God Is Too Small* (New York: Macmillan, 1985).